PRAISE FOR *THE SMART PERFORMANCE BOOK*

"The world is full of self-assessment tools, but few are simple, relatable and linked so directly to actions which will quickly enhance skills. Genius."
OLLIE JOYCE, Global Chief Transformation Officer, Mindshare

"A gem of a book – it distils a lifetime of business learning into a series of practical ideas."
RICHARD SHOTTON, Author, *The Illusion of Choice* and *The Choice Factory*

"Fast learning for the modern age."
JANET UTTLEY, Head of Industry Development, VisitEngland

"Finally, a down-to-earth roadmap to becoming better at almost everything."
JOHN V. PETROCELLI, Author, *The Life-Changing Science of Detecting Bullshit*

"This is a brilliant system for assessing teams and helping anyone improve their skills."
CHRIS HIRST, Author, *No Bullshit Leadership* and *No Bullshit Change*

"In a tech-dominated world, it's easy to overlook the most valuable driver of growth – teamwork. This book is what we all need to understand how the needs of individuals and companies come together to create high-performing teams and rewarding work experiences for all."
JAMES SHORELAND, CEO, VCCP Media

"Marx criticised philosophers on the basis that they only described the world – the point being to change it. Too many performance and coaching texts offer one without the other. This is a brilliant integration of the no matter what
MARK EARLS, Author, *Herd*, *I'll Have Wh*

T0370935

Published by
LID Publishing
An imprint of LID Business Media Ltd.
LABS House, 15–19 Bloomsbury Way,
London, WC1A 2TH, UK

info@lidpublishing.com
www.lidpublishing.com

A member of:

businesspublishersroundtable.com

The ACES System® is a registered UK trademark of Expert Advice Limited
and held at the Intellectual Property Office in the United Kingdom.
Trade Mark No. UK00003870556.
Big thanks to Dave Hart for all the tech work on the ACES system.

Printed and bound in Great Britain by Halstan Ltd.

ISBN: 978-1-915951-65-6
ISBN: 978-1-915951-66-3 (ebook)

Cover and page design: Caroline Li

THE SMART PERFORMANCE BOOK

HOW TO BE YOUR BEST BUSINESS SELF

KEVIN DUNCAN
SARAH DUNCAN

MADRID | MEXICO CITY | LONDON
BUENOS AIRES | BOGOTA | SHANGHAI

FOR OTHER TITLES
IN THE SERIES ...

CONCISE
ADVICE
LAB

SMALL
BOOKS:
BIG
IDEAS

CLEVER CONTENT, DYNAMIC IDEAS, PRACTICAL
SOLUTIONS AND ENGAGING VISUALS –
A CATALYST TO INSPIRE NEW WAYS OF THINKING
AND PROBLEM-SOLVING IN A COMPLEX WORLD

www.lidpublishing.com/product-category/concise-advice-series

CONTENTS

INTRODUCTION

This book is, in many respects, the culmination of a lifetime's work.

If that sounds a bit grand, it draws together all the best bits of everything we have learned in business in the last 40 years.

During that time, we have read over 500 business books and summarised each on a page. Then we wrote a set of Concise Advice books that encapsulate the best thinking in them.

We then trained over 20,000 people, which allowed us to understand the most important capabilities that people need to be effective in business.

We distilled this into eight performance areas: attitude, action, creativity, communication, efficiency, empathy, strategy and sustainability.

We then invented a fast self-audit, which tells you your typology and signposts you to microlearning specific to your needs.

Having made all that work online, we were then asked to write a book about it, and here it is.

The book is intended to provide a gateway to perpetual learning. You can brush up skills in a specific area or mix and match.

You can test yourself again and see how your skills have developed.

Keen students can follow lines of inquiry right back to their source by accessing our other books, or the 100 books in the further reading suggestions.

Each provocation shows the book that inspired it, asks you to consider three pointed questions so you can improve how you approach issues, and allows you to pursue your thinking further.

The learning never ends, and even our take on our own material has evolved since we wrote the original books.

As a B Corp, our purpose is to create, educate and donate.

We support the philosophy of continuous learning.

That's what this book is all about.

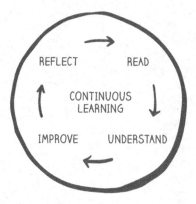

Kevin and Sarah Duncan
Westminster, 2024

"

**Start where you are.
Use what you have.
Do what you can.**

"

Arthur Ashe,
Tennis player

PART ONE

BACKGROUND TO THE BOOK AND THE ACES SYSTEM®

1. WHAT IS SMART PERFORMANCE?

Smart performance means having a broad range of skills that enable you to be a success. It's not enough to be good at just one thing. You don't have to be top at everything, but the broader the range of your skills, the better you are likely to perform.

Successful modern businesses need to harness a broad spectrum of skills and people, and that means they need you at your best. At the heart of this book is the ACES System – a diagnostic tool that enables you to assess your personal strengths and identify self-improvement areas to help you succeed in the modern business world.

It covers every aspect of high-functioning business performance, from attitude, action, creativity and communication to efficiency, empathy, strategy and sustainability. In short, it ensures that you can be your best, get along with people and get ahead.

Smart performance is not about being competitive or winning. It requires social intelligence as well as good technical skills. It requires you to be inquisitive and thoughtful, taking a responsible approach to learning and self-improvement. The more you discover, the better you will feel and the better you will perform.

2. WHAT IS THE ACES SYSTEM?

The ACES System shows you how to be your best business self. It asks ten carefully conceived questions in eight skills areas, which enables you to discover your typology based on the 56 possible permutations. Yours is formulated based on your top strength and your second best. This then signposts you to the relevant sections in the book. All of this can also be done online.

Training over 20,000 people has allowed us to identify skills capabilities in these eight important areas. There are 56 possible combinations, based on the relationship between these primary and secondary skills.

The system puts the power in the hands of the individual. It celebrates self-assessment by allowing you to summarise your own skills rather than succumb to an arbitrary construct imposed upon you. So you don't need to wonder whether you are being subjected to trick questions or questionable profiling techniques.

The ACES acronym is derived from the eight skills areas:
A = Attitude and Action
C = Creativity and Communication
E = Efficiency and Empathy
S = Strategy and Sustainability

"

Excellence is perseverance in disguise.

"

Katie Boulter,
Tennis player

PART TWO

THE ACES SYSTEM
IN DETAIL AND
HOW TO USE IT

1. THE EIGHT SKILLS AREAS

The eight skills areas have been researched and analysed over 25 years of training 20,000 people. They cover the main capabilities that people need in order to be successful at work.

ATTITUDE — This is all about being a self-starter. The individual is already motivated and doesn't need constant prompting from others.

ACTION — This is all about being an enactor who is instinctively action-orientated. These people are really good at getting things done.

CREATIVITY — This is all about being an inventor. The person is naturally creative, inventive, and constantly coming up with new ideas.

COMMUNICATION — This is all about being an excellent communicator. Such people tend to be naturally persuasive and have mastered a range of techniques for getting their point across well.

EFFICIENCY — This is all about being a brilliant organiser. The individual is highly productive and always makes best use of time, taking the path of least resistance.

EMPATHY — This is all about being a good listener. Such people are always thoughtful and take care to pay significant attention to the views of others.

STRATEGY — This is all about being a superb strategist. This individual really knows the difference between a properly thought-through approach as opposed to a quick tactic.

SUSTAINABILITY — This is all about being a long-termist. These people are highly responsible and take great care to consider the future and the implications of actions taken now.

2. THE 80 STATEMENTS

Before you answer the self-audit, here are some notes to help you get the most out of it.

- This is not a psychometric test. It does not ask trick questions and it does not force you into an A/B answer.
- If you answer the same number to every question in a section, you will generate a result with no variation, so try to avoid doing that.
- Try to avoid scoring yourself with a middling three too often. You can if you want, but it is better to go higher or lower to create relative differences.
- Don't worry about overscoring or underscoring. Some people give themselves a five for a skill; others would give themselves a lower score.
- Don't compare yourself to others as you complete the audit. It's about the relative difference between your own skills, not a competition with others.
- Most of the questions are based on being a member of staff working in a salaried company. If you are self-employed or in different circumstances, don't worry. Just use your skill and judgement.
- There is no endgame other than suggested areas for self-improvement, signposting you to helpful learning content.

ATTITUDE STATEMENTS

ATTITUDE

Give yourself a score out of 5

| 1 | 2 | 3 | 4 | 5 |

Strongly disagree   Strongly agree

I am prepared to put the necessary effort in to create opportunities.

I am prepared to challenge my old habits and behaviours.

I have long-term resilience and am able to stick with projects.

I can turn frightening things into opportunities.

I own up when something goes wrong and then seek advice.

I understand that other people may be less enthusiastic about what I am doing than I am.

I am able to pause and reflect on my work from time to time.

I am prepared to ditch projects that are OK, but not great, to improve quality.

I use solitude for productive thinking time.

I deliberately break my routine from time to time to keep things fresh.

OVERALL SCORE (total divided by 10)

Add up your total score and divide it by 10 to reveal your average.

ACTION STATEMENTS

Give yourself a score out of 5

| 1 | 2 | 3 | 4 | 5 |

Strongly disagree   Strongly agree

I remove distractions and interference to improve my concentration levels.

I look at what is possible rather than wild, impractical ideas.

I am able to prioritise tasks and concentrate on what is truly essential.

I can abandon an idea if it doesn't fit the task properly.

I prefer acting to just talking about things.

I am good at distinguishing between high and low priority projects.

I consistently meet my deadlines.

I am good at ensuring momentum on initiatives once they are started.

I am good at admitting when approaches are not working.

I thoughtfully consider a wide range of options before deciding on a course of action.

OVERALL SCORE (total divided by 10)

Add up your total score and divide it by 10 to reveal your average.

CREATIVITY STATEMENTS

CREATIVITY

Give yourself a score out of 5

| 1 | 2 | 3 | 4 | 5 |

Strongly disagree   Strongly agree

I am able to combine commercial realism with the creative process from the start.

I always make sure that the objective or brief is clear before idea generation begins.

I always assess the true complexity of a creative challenge before generating ideas.

I trust my mind to arrive at intelligent solutions eventually.

I look beyond the category in which I operate to inspire new ideas.

I am prepared to drop ideas and projects that aren't showing sufficient progress.

I am good at reducing a large number of ideas down to a manageable number.

I allow ideas to develop and flourish before killing them off too quickly.

I have a good track record of predicting ideas that will be successful.

I am able to generate inspiring ideas that people get excited about.

OVERALL SCORE (total divided by 10)

Add up your total score and divide it by 10 to reveal your average.

COMMUNICATION STATEMENTS

COMMUNICATION

Give yourself a score out of 5

| 1 | 2 | 3 | 4 | 5 |

Strongly disagree   Strongly agree

I don't embark on presentations until I have a clear point of view and a persuasive line of argument.

My formal presentations are clear and concise.

I use a mix of visual and verbal methods to accommodate a broad range of audiences.

My written communications are always as short and concise as possible.

I avoid cliché and corporate jargon.

I always make sure that something has been achieved before making claims.

I believe that listening is a vital element of successful communication.

I am good at the art of negotiation.

I think things through clearly, but don't overthink them.

In the event of any miscommunication, I learn from my mistakes.

OVERALL SCORE (total divided by 10)

Add up your total score and divide it by 10 to reveal your average.

EFFICIENCY STATEMENTS

Give yourself a score out of 5

1	2	3	4	5

Strongly disagree   Strongly agree

I set realistic targets.

I deliver on my plans.

I put consistent effort into everything I do.

I regularly review my ways of working.

I am good at identifying what is truly possible.

I empower myself and colleagues to challenge and improve ways of working.

I am good at prioritising tasks.

I actively take responsibility for my projects.

I give colleagues and teams regular and appropriate feedback about their work.

I remove distractions and interference to improve my concentration levels.

OVERALL SCORE (total divided by 10)

Add up your total score and divide it by 10 to reveal your average.

EMPATHY STATEMENTS

EMPATHY

Give yourself a score out of 5

| 1 | 2 | 3 | 4 | 5 |

Strongly disagree   Strongly agree

I always foster a culture of trust and teamwork.

I recognise that my day-to-day behaviour helps shape the culture of the company I am in.

I can spot dysfunction in teams and I always work to improve matters.

I am strongly supportive of my company's diversity and inclusion efforts and initiatives.

I am comfortable working with people whose approaches are very different to mine.

I always create an environment that is conducive to generating a diverse range of opinions.

I seek advice from outside my normal peer group to broaden my perspective.

I adjust my language to communicate with people in the most inclusive and empathetic way.

I encourage people around me to pursue things that they feel strongly about.

I actively support charitable activities.

OVERALL SCORE (total divided by 10)

Add up your total score and divide it by 10 to reveal your average.

STRATEGY STATEMENTS

STRATEGY

Give yourself a score out of 5

1	2	3	4	5

Strongly disagree   Strongly agree

I have a clear understanding of what a strategy is.

I make a clear distinction between overall strategy and specific tactics.

I know the difference between a strategy and a plan.

I know the difference between a strategy and a financial target.

I know how to create a commercial strategy.

I understand that selling isn't just for salespeople.

I take strategy seriously.

I believe that customers need to be at the heart of any strategy.

I am familiar with the principles of creating a people strategy.

I can switch between the big picture and specific actions without micromanaging the detail.

OVERALL SCORE (total divided by 10)

Add up your total score and divide it by 10 to reveal your average.

SUSTAINABILITY STATEMENTS

Give yourself a score out of 5

| 1 | 2 | 3 | 4 | 5 |

Strongly disagree   Strongly agree

I fully understand the implications of climate change.

I understand my own carbon footprint.

I am familiar with the global ambitions relating to sustainability.

I understand why sustainability is important to business performance.

I believe business exists for more than just the pursuit of profit.

I try not to put short-term gain ahead of long-term sustainable development.

Having a strong moral purpose is important to me.

I am familiar with the principles of the circular economy.

I believe that sustainability is everyone's responsibility.

I am conscious of greenwashing, both in terms of my own company's products and when buying products from other people.

OVERALL SCORE (total divided by 10)

Add up your total score and divide it by 10 to reveal your average.

Now transfer your overall score from each of the eight skills areas and put them in the appropriate box. Identify your top score and your second highest and transfer them to the bottom panel. In the unlikely event of a dead heat, look at whichever typology describes you best.

YOUR SCORES

ATTITUDE

ACTION

CREATIVITY

COMMUNICATION

EFFICIENCY

EMPATHY

STRATEGY

SUSTAINABILITY

Fill in your top and second highest score.

My TOP SCORE is:

My SECOND HIGHEST SCORE is:

Now use the grid to reveal your ACES typology.

Take your top score on the top horizontal line to identify your primary skill.

Follow the grid downward to match it with your secondary skill on the left-hand vertical axis.

Note the typology abbreviation and find the full typology name in the list on page 24.

		HIGHEST SCORE - PRIMARY							
---	---	ATTITUDE	ACTION	CREATIVITY	COMMUNICATION	EFFICIENCY	EMPATHY	STRATEGY	SUSTAINABILITY
SECOND HIGHEST SCORE - SECONDARY	ATTITUDE		ME	MI	MC	MO	ML	MS	MLT
	ACTION	AOSS		AOI	AOC	AOO	AOL	AOS	AOLT
	CREATIVITY	CSS	CE		CC	CO	CL	CS	CLT
	COMMUNICATION	PeSS	PeE	PeI		PeO	PeL	PeS	PeLT
	EFFICIENCY	PrSS	PrE	PrI	PrC		PrL	PrS	PrLT
	EMPATHY	TSS	TE	TI	TC	TO		TS	TLT
	STRATEGY	SSS	SE	SI	SC	SO	SL		SLT
	SUSTAINABILITY	RSS	RE	RI	RC	RO	RL	RS	

AOC	= Action-Orientated Communicator	**PrC**	= Productive Communicator
AOI	= Action-Orientated Inventor	**PrE**	= Productive Enactor
AOL	= Action-Orientated Listener	**PrI**	= Productive Inventor
AOLT	= Action-Orientated Long-Termist	**PrL**	= Productive Listener
AOO	= Action-Orientated Organiser	**PrLT**	= Productive Long-Termist
AOSS	= Action-Orientated Self-Starter	**PrSS**	= Productive Self-Starter
AOS	= Action-Orientated Strategist	**PrS**	= Productive Strategist
CC	= Creative Communicator	**RC**	= Responsible Communicator
CE	= Creative Enactor	**RE**	= Responsible Enactor
CL	= Creative Listener	**RI**	= Responsible Inventor
CLT	= Creative Long-Termist	**RL**	= Responsible Listener
CO	= Creative Organiser	**RO**	= Responsible Organiser
CSS	= Creative Self-Starter	**RSS**	= Responsible Self-Starter
CS	= Creative Strategist	**RS**	= Responsible Strategist
MC	= Motivated Communicator	**SC**	= Strategic Communicator
ME	= Motivated Enactor	**SE**	= Strategic Enactor
MI	= Motivated Inventor	**SI**	= Strategic Inventor
ML	= Motivated Listener	**SL**	= Strategic Listener
MLT	= Motivated Long-Termist	**SLT**	= Strategic Long-Termist
MO	= Motivated Organiser	**SO**	= Strategic Organiser
MS	= Motivated Strategist	**SSS**	= Strategic Self-Starter
PeE	= Persuasive Enactor	**TC**	= Thoughtful Communicator
PeI	= Persuasive Inventor	**TE**	= Thoughtful Enactor
PeL	= Persuasive Listener	**TI**	= Thoughtful Inventor
PeLT	= Persuasive Long-Termist	**TLT**	= Thoughtful Long-Termist
PeO	= Persuasive Organiser	**TO**	= Thoughtful Organiser
PeSS	= Persuasive Self-Starter	**TSS**	= Thoughtful Self-Starter
PeS	= Persuasive Strategist	**TS**	= Thoughtful Strategist

Turn to the list of all 56 typologies to find an additional descriptor of
what your typology means in a little more detail.

3. THE 56 TYPOLOGIES

Each typology is based on the interrelationship between your top score and your second best. This generates a two-word typology, such as **Productive Inventor**, and a one-sentence descriptor, such as *You are a master of getting stuff done, but with creative flair.*

THE 56 TYPOLOGY DESCRIPTORS IN ALPHABETICAL ORDER

Action-Orientated Communicator (AOC)
You are excellent at communicating and want to see action taken as a result.

Action-Orientated Inventor (AOI)
You have ideas and get on with them without needing to be asked.

Action-Orientated Listener (AOL)
You are good at weighing situations and then getting on with solutions straightaway.

Action-Orientated Long-Termist (AOLT)
You care about developing business in a sustainable way and are good at getting done what needs to be done.

Action-Orientated Organiser (AOO)
You get things done and don't need to be chased to do them.

Action-Orientated Self-Starter (AOSS)
You don't need to be asked to get things done. You just do it.

Action-Orientated Strategist (AOS)
You are something of a rare breed – a thinker who also naturally takes action.

Creative Communicator (CC)
You are adept at convincing and explaining, as well as coming up with ideas.

Creative Enactor (CE)
You have a powerful combination of coming up with ideas and getting them done.

Creative Listener (CL)
You consider the points of view of others before coming up with strong ideas.

Creative Long-Termist (CLT)
You care about developing business in a sustainable way and are good at coming up with smart ideas to improve the future.

Creative Organiser (CO)
You are a master of getting stuff done, but with creative flair.

Creative Self-Starter (CSS)
You have the discipline to see ideas through, as well as create them.

Creative Strategist (CS)
You think very carefully and broadly before coming up with ideas.

Motivated Communicator (MC)
You can convey ideas and information well and are well motivated to do them.

Motivated Enactor (ME)
You are all about getting things done.

Motivated Inventor (MI)
You are naturally predisposed to come up with ideas.

Motivated Listener (ML)
You are good at weighing up situations and then approaching them in an intelligent way.

Motivated Long-Termist (MLT)
You care deeply about the long term and have a can-do approach to what needs to be done.

Motivated Organiser (MO)
You are adept at getting things done and enjoy having a can-do disposition.

Motivated Strategist (MS)
You don't need others to force you to think deeply and are naturally inclined to get on with thoughtful work all the time.

Persuasive Enactor (PeE)
You want things to happen as a result of what you say.

Persuasive Inventor (PeI)
You are able to both come up with ideas and explain them convincingly.

Persuasive Listener (PeL)
You sympathise with your audience in an engaging and inclusive way.

Persuasive Long-Termist (PeLT)
You care deeply about the long term and are good at explaining the challenges and ideas that will affect the future.

Persuasive Organiser (PeO)
You get things done and then explain the results very clearly.

Persuasive Self-Starter (PeSS)
You are naturally inclined to communicate effectively and don't need to be forced to do it.

Persuasive Strategist (PeS)
You think very carefully about issues first and are then good at explaining them to people.

Productive Communicator (PrC)
You are good at explaining what needs to be done, as well as identifying how to do it in the most efficient way.

Productive Enactor (PrE)
You always get things done in the most effective way.

Productive Inventor (PrI)
You come up with ideas and are able to understand how to execute them efficiently.

Productive Listener (PrL)
You are able to assess challenges in a well-balanced way and work out the simplest, most effective way to proceed.

Productive Long-Termist (PrLT)
You care about developing business in a sustainable way and can see the easiest ways forward to improve things in the future.

Productive Self-Starter (PrSS)
You are hard-wired to just get things done without anyone chasing you.

Productive Strategist (PrS)
You excel at looking at a wide range of options before determining the most effective way forward.

Responsible Communicator (RC)
You are convincing when explaining problems that require long-lasting solutions.

Responsible Enactor (RE)
You can identify quick wins that have a long-lasting effect.

Responsible Inventor (RI)
You can generate ideas that solve complex and enduring problems.

Responsible Listener (RL)
You are able to assess challenges and assimilate the views of others before proposing long-lasting solutions.

Responsible Organiser (RO)
You are good at identifying the simplest way to approach problems that require long-lasting solutions.

Responsible Self-Starter (RSS)
You are naturally inclined to take personal responsibility for the long term.

Responsible Strategist (RS)
You thoughtfully review all possible ways forward and view them through the eyes of a long-term guardian.

Strategic Communicator (SC)
You are good at getting people to agree that your proposed strategic approach is right.

Strategic Enactor (SE)
You approach strategy with pragmatism.

Strategic Inventor (SI)
You have an interesting combination of coming up with ideas and seeing their strategic application. A rare breed.

Strategic Listener (SL)
You consider many points of view before coming up with strategic recommendations.

Strategic Long-Termist (SLT)
You care about developing business in a sustainable way and are very good at envisaging strategic approaches that will be effective and enduring.

Strategic Organiser (SO)
You are good at seeing the simplest way through but in a thoughtful, strategic way rather than a tactical quick fix.

Strategic Self-Starter (SSS)
You don't need persuading to think deeply about important issues.

Thoughtful Communicator (TC)
You are very good at communicating, but also prepared to hear alternative views.

Thoughtful Enactor (TE)
You get things done whist making sure that they involve others on the way.

Thoughtful Inventor (TI)
You can come up with ideas but are prepared to listen to the views of others about them.

Thoughtful Long-Termist (TLT)
You care deeply about the long term and are good at paying attention to the views of others to broaden the collective perspective.

Thoughtful Organiser (TO)
You achieve a lot and are prepared to pay attention to alternative ways of doing things.

Thoughtful Self-Starter (TSS)
You are naturally driven and able to pay attention to others and give them your time.

Thoughtful Strategist (TS)
You are a deep thinker who also pays attention to the views of others.

Now go back to page 22 and remind yourself of your weakest areas.

Head to the relevant parts of the book for immediate learning material and start improving your skills.

TAKE THE TEST ONLINE

You can also take the test online. Your summarised typology and signposted priority microlearning PDF (including audio options) will arrive instantly in your inbox – see opposite.

For a special discount, go to:

expertadviceonline.com/smartperformance

Your answers to The ACES System®
questions show your current typology as:

Thoughtful Inventor

You come up with great ideas and are prepared to listen to the views of others about them.

Example from the online version with interactive tabs

ATTITUDE

These are your top three improvement areas in ATTITUDE. As a matter of priority,
look at these. Click Read, Listen, or Link to access or download improvement material.

	Score	Download Improvement Material (1-2 mins each)	Listen	Read
I am prepared to put the necessary effort in to create opportunities.	1	Effort Creates Opportunity	▶	PDF
I am prepared to challenge my old habits and behaviours.	1	Letting Go	▶	PDF
I have long-term resilience and am able to stick with projects.	1	Sticking at it	▶	PDF

Here are the rest of your scores with more improvement material. The related reading panel
takes you to one-page summaries of other books on the topic to widen your learning.

	Score	Download Improvement Material (1-2 mins each)	Listen	Read
I can turn frightening things into opportunities.	2	Turning Fear Into Success	▶	PDF
I own up when something goes wrong and then seek advice.	2	Confess and Consult	▶	PDF
I understand that other people may be less enthusiastic about what I am doing than I am.	3	Curb Your Enthusiasm	▶	PDF
I am able to pause and reflect on my work from time to time.	3	Pause For Thought	▶	PDF
I am prepared to ditch projects that are OK, but not great, to improve qaulity.	4	Keep The Best, Bin The Rest	▶	PDF
I use solitude for productive thinking time.	4	How To Think Alone	▶	PDF
I deliberately break my routine from time to time to keep things fresh.	4	Keeping It Fresh	▶	PDF

Other Related Book Summaries (2-3 mins each)	Link
Decisive, Heath & Heath	→
Drive, Dan Pink	→
Flow, Csikszentmihalyi	→
Leaders Eat Last, Sinek	→
The E Myth Revisited, Gerber	→

"

Whatever inspiration is, it's born from a continuous 'I don't know.'

"

Wislawa Szymborska,
Poet and Nobel prize winner

PART THREE

SELF-IMPROVEMENT
MATERIAL

1. ATTITUDE

> *"I'm not conceited – I'm convinced."*
> Little Richard

Very little works well if your attitude isn't right.

We start by explaining the link between effort and opportunity and the need to let go of old, unhelpful habits.

We move on to persistence and how to deal with scary situations by turning them to your advantage.

When you do mess up, there are excellent coping strategies at your disposal, and we explain how to balance your own enthusiasm with what others are interested in.

We finish off with how to ensure the highest quality in your work, allowing yourself to pause and think regularly, and keeping everything fresh with regular mental reinvention.

I am prepared to put the necessary effort in to create opportunities. > EFFORT CREATES OPPORTUNITY	1.1
I am prepared to challenge my old habits and behaviours. > LETTING GO	1.2
I have long-term resilience and am able to stick with projects. > STICKING AT IT	1.3
I can turn frightening things into opportunities. > TURNING FEAR INTO SUCCESS	1.4
I own up when something goes wrong and then seek advice. > CONFESS AND CONSULT	1.5
I understand that other people may be less enthusiastic about what I am doing than I am. > CURB YOUR ENTHUSIASM	1.6
I am able to pause and reflect on my work from time to time. > PAUSE FOR THOUGHT	1.7
I am prepared to ditch projects that are OK, but not great, to improve quality. > KEEP THE BEST, BIN THE REST	1.8
I use solitude for productive thinking time. > HOW TO THINK ALONE	1.9
I deliberately break my routine from time to time to keep things fresh. > KEEPING IT FRESH	1.10

ATTITUDE

ACTION

CREATIVITY

COMMUNICATION

EFFICIENCY

EMPATHY

STRATEGY

SUSTAINABILITY

1.1 EFFORT CREATES OPPORTUNITY

I am prepared to put the necessary effort in to create opportunities.

> *"Opportunity is missed by most people because it is dressed in overalls and looks like work."*
> Thomas Edison

The American inventor Thomas Edison was also the man behind *"Genius is 1% inspiration and 99% perspiration"* and *"I have not failed. I've just found 10,000 ways that won't work."*

People love the idea of being successful. They crave achievement but often are simply in love with the idea of the result. They want the reward but, in truth, they just aren't prepared to put in the work to get there.

To create opportunities and achieve more of what you want, your approach needs to involve applied effort. So, how can we make what we want more achievable? First, we need to *know* what we want. Then, we need to work out the small and manageable steps that will get us there, taking a lofty and potentially overwhelming goal and breaking it down into clear, bite-size tasks.

Each time we take another step toward our goal by fulfilling a task, we are motivating ourselves through that achievement. It becomes a self-motivating cycle.

Consider this
- Do you know what you want?
- Can you put in the work to succeed?
- What steps will get you there?

Inspired by *The Excellence Book*

ATTITUDE

ACTION

CREATIVITY

COMMUNICATION

EFFICIENCY

EMPATHY

STRATEGY

SUSTAINABILITY

1.2 LETTING GO

I am prepared to challenge my old habits and behaviours.

On 1 December 1862, President Abraham Lincoln delivered his annual message to Congress. The country was in the middle of a civil war. This is how he concluded.

> *"The dogmas of the quiet past are inadequate to the stormy present. The occasion is piled high with difficulty, and we must rise with the occasion. As our case is new, so we must think anew, and act anew. We must disenthrall ourselves, and then we shall save our country."*
> Abraham Lincoln

Disenthrall. It's an interesting word. To enthrall means to capture someone's attention. This could be good or bad, depending on what exactly is attracting your undivided attention. To disenthrall means to discharge, free, emancipate, liberate, loosen, release, unbind, uncage, unchain or unfetter.

So, if you are obsessed with perpetually doing or seeing things in a certain way, you may first need to disenthrall yourself to stand any chance of changing your attitude. Only then will you have a chance of seeing other possibilities.

In order to change any of our own habits and behaviours, we must first become aware of them. From this perspective, we can analyse whether that's how we would, or wouldn't, like to respond to any given situation.

Next time you find yourself reacting badly, note down what happened and how you behaved. When you have some time for reflection, look at this from an outsider's perspective. What were your triggers? What can you learn about yourself from this situation and ultimately change?

Consider this
- Can you disenthrall yourself?
- Can you change the way you normally do things?
- Can you think of a new and better way?

Inspired by *The Excellence Book*

ATTITUDE

ACTION

CREATIVITY

COMMUNICATION

EFFICIENCY

EMPATHY

STRATEGY

SUSTAINABILITY

1.3 STICKING AT IT

I have long-term resilience and am able to stick with projects.

Resilience in the face of adversity is a vital trait. Life is not a smooth road. In fact, if it were, most of us would be bored. As noted by Max McKeown in his book, *#Now*, those confronted by extremely tricky obstacles such as cancer are said to have a *feisty spirit of survivorship*.

It's a laughing-is-winning approach, and this is something that can be adopted by anyone, including those facing life-threatening circumstances. This transformative ability to make good things happen through a positive attitude is a quality you can discover in yourself. We can draw inspiration here from the famous mountaineer Edmund Hillary.

> *"It is not the mountain we conquer but ourselves."*
> Edmund Hillary

It's all about taking control of your attitude to life: one person's adversity is another's inspiration. It is not easy to get back up once we've been knocked down. But if we never get back up again, we will never get anywhere. Absolutely everybody fails at some point, some more than others.

It's our attitude to failure, and cultivating resilience, that allow us to strive and continue. So, when you face a setback (which you will), take some time afterward to take stock. What did you learn from the experience? Can you learn from it, or reframe it and see it as a positive?

Consider this
- Do you have a feisty spirit?
- Can you stick at things?
- Can you laugh in the face of adversity?

Inspired by *The Excellence Book*

ATTITUDE

ACTION

CREATIVITY

COMMUNICATION

EFFICIENCY

EMPATHY

STRATEGY

SUSTAINABILITY

1.4 TURNING FEAR INTO SUCCESS

I can turn frightening things into opportunities.

> *"Fear is wisdom in the face of danger. It's nothing to be ashamed of."*
> Sherlock Holmes

This is from the book *The Abominable Bride*. It's OK to be afraid. In fact, it's often beneficial. Animals have a clearly demarcated sense of flight or fight. And it's driven by fright, which is a sudden, intense feeling of fear.

So being scared can be extremely beneficial for survival or progress. Not so that you are petrified into nonaction. But so that you fully appreciate the possibilities that may follow from your actions. Harness the fear to anticipate what to do next.

Flight could allow you to fight another day. A fight should only be considered if you are convinced you can win. Confront the initial fear and turn it into a wise attitude.

Fear is a natural reaction to the unknown because it keeps us alert for dangers that arise from new situations. This means that every new venture will come with a healthy dollop of apprehension.

We cannot get rid of fear, but we can learn to accept it. And each time you overcome it, you will learn not to be afraid of a new situation. Ask yourself what you can do that is just out of your comfort zone.

Consider this
- Are you afraid to be afraid?
- Do you accept that fear can be helpful?
- Can you use fear to inform the best response?

Inspired by *The Excellence Book*

ATTITUDE

ACTION

CREATIVITY

COMMUNICATION

EFFICIENCY

EMPATHY

STRATEGY

SUSTAINABILITY

1.5 CONFESS AND CONSULT

I own up when something goes wrong and then seek advice.

Student pilots are taught early in their training what to do if they get into trouble.

1. *Climb*: get yourself out of danger immediately by increasing altitude.

2. *Confess*: talk to the control tower and explain what the problem is.

3. *Comply*: do exactly what you are told by the air traffic controller.

Climb, confess, comply is a useful attitude when dealing with awkward circumstances. So the next time you are out of your depth, admit it immediately, ask for help quickly, and then do exactly what it takes to resolve the situation. Don't dig a deeper hole or paint yourself into a corner. Climb, confess, comply.

We can predict that something, at some point, will go wrong. This is not designed to scare you, but rather to prepare you. It happens to all of us, no matter who we are. Remember that it's not personal.

Whenever you do fail, give it your best shot not to let it define you. By sharing the issue and working through it, you aren't suffering alone. When you last failed, how did you handle it?

Consider this
- Do you confess when you have messed up?
- Do you comply with advice immediately?
- Can you react differently next time?

Inspired by *The Excellence Book*

ATTITUDE

ACTION

CREATIVITY

COMMUNICATION

EFFICIENCY

EMPATHY

STRATEGY

SUSTAINABILITY

1.6 CURB YOUR ENTHUSIASM

I understand that other people may be less enthusiastic about what I am doing than I am.

In his memoirs, *Gig: The Life and Times of a Rock-star Fantasist*, British poet Simon Armitage recalls returning to his hometown. There, in the bargain bin of a second-hand bookshop, he found a copy of one of his own books. It was inscribed in the front, in his own handwriting, *"To Mum and Dad."* Despite their son pouring his best efforts into having a book published, his parents obviously didn't consider it worth keeping.

Which just goes to show that however much you care about something, other people probably don't. In fact, they might not even be interested. One person's passion may be another's ambivalence. It's up to you to decide what you feel strongly about. But don't expect anyone else to care. Do your parents really understand what you do for a living?

The Spotlight Effect is a psychological concept in which we overestimate how much others are focused on us. In reality, everyone's spotlight is on themselves. It's highly likely that, when you think you're being judged, your companion is busy thinking the same thing about themselves. In the kindest way, no one is giving you as much attention as you think.

Consider this
- Do you assume that everyone else is interested?
- Can you retain your own level of personal focus?
- Do you often think you're being judged?

Inspired by *The Excellence Book*

ATTITUDE

ACTION

CREATIVITY

COMMUNICATION

EFFICIENCY

EMPATHY

STRATEGY

SUSTAINABILITY

1.7 PAUSE FOR THOUGHT

I am able to pause and reflect on my work from time to time.

> "All of man's misery comes from his incapacity to sit alone in an empty, quiet room."
> Blaise Pascal

Blaise Pascal was a French mathematician. He said that we are useless at doing nothing, but when we rush into things, we usually cause trouble for ourselves and for others. In his book, *An Optimist's Tour of the Future*, Mark Stevenson relates a story told by Tim Langley, director of charcoal manufacturer Carbonscape.

An elderly German businessman and his wife hired his boat to go looking for dolphins. There were none to be found, but he kept pushing Tim to keep looking.

Eventually after two hours, Tim asked: *"Do you want to continue looking, or do you just want to sit and be?"*

Such an idea had never occurred to the German. In order to determine a decent attitude, we need to pause and think properly. Sometimes we just need to sit and be. We cannot 'do' all the time. Excess productivity leads to burnout, which, in turn, forces us to do nothing, as we are no longer capable.

To have the energy to do things well, we need rest. Rest brings us down from a doing, adrenal, fight-or-flight state into a calming, rest-and-digest state. In this state we get better sleep, which means our cells regenerate properly and prepare us better for the next day. Recharging is, therefore, essential to being a healthy human being.

Consider this
- Can you just sit and be?
- Can you just pause and think?
- Do you pause before you act?

Inspired by *The Excellence Book*

ATTITUDE

ACTION

CREATIVITY

COMMUNICATION

EFFICIENCY

EMPATHY

STRATEGY

SUSTAINABILITY

1.8 KEEP THE BEST, BIN THE REST

I am prepared to ditch projects that are OK, but not great, to improve quality.

Having the right attitude means exercising task triage. That means distinguishing between a smart idea that is impracticable and one that is good and can genuinely be done. Most projects fall into two categories:

1. Not that exciting.
2. Exciting, but unrealistic to implement.

A good project is both exciting and doable. Jerome was a very brainy priest, theologian and historian who lived around the year 400 CE and translated the Bible into Latin. His personal mantra was this.

> *"Good, better, best*
> *Never let it rest*
> *Til your good is better*
> *And your better is best."*
> Jerome

In other words, keep only the best, and bin the rest. It's the only way to keep quality and productivity at its highest level. By focusing on fewer tasks, we give each of them more energy, time and effort. This will naturally produce better results. As well as better results, you will become more knowledgeable on each subject you concentrate on.

This will lead to consistently better outcomes based on a clear attitude. To enact this, we need to give ourselves the time and space to focus. This means cutting unnecessary things from our daily tasks or delegating them to someone else. Look at your to-do list. What can you get rid of or delegate so that you have a clear focus?

Consider this
- Do you struggle to get things done?
- Do you go for high quality?
- Do you throw out substandard stuff?

Inspired by *The Excellence Book*

ATTITUDE

ACTION

CREATIVITY

COMMUNICATION

EFFICIENCY

EMPATHY

STRATEGY

SUSTAINABILITY

1.9 HOW TO THINK ALONE

I use solitude for productive thinking time.

According to Agnes Martin, the American abstract painter: *The best things in life happen when you're alone.* Working together is great, but the principle of collaboration is often abused.

Many executives get a lot more done at home than in the office. That's because they have uninterrupted time to think and do. There's little worse than someone dumping all their random thoughts on you, hoping you will sort out their thinking for them.

It is everyone's responsibility to think as hard as possible about an issue before burdening someone else with half-baked ideas. Solitude enables you to get your thoughts together. So, use thoughtful time alone as a springboard for a better approach. As the guitarist and singer Chrissie Hynde points out: *Being alone is underrated.*

The Empath's Survival Guide, by Judith Orloff, explains that solitude is necessary to recover and regroup, and that taking time away from other people is essential to rebalance your own energy. This is especially true for empaths who are on the more sensitive end of the spectrum. Being alone will help us recharge but is also a sign of contentment because being comfortable in our own skin is the ultimate self-compliment.

Consider this
- Can you think alone?
- Do you create time and space to think?
- Do you give your brain a chance to think properly?

Inspired by *The Excellence Book*

ATTITUDE

ACTION

CREATIVITY

COMMUNICATION

EFFICIENCY

EMPATHY

STRATEGY

SUSTAINABILITY

1.10 KEEPING IT FRESH

I deliberately break my routine from time to time to keep things fresh.

If you keep doing the same old thing, then you'll just be doing, well, the same old thing. Such consistency may be admirable in some spheres, but in most instances, you will want to progress. Most humans become bored easily. So, if things have become repetitive, it may be time to make some changes.

Alter the pattern. Take some measured risks. Live a little. This is what Paulo Coelho, the Brazilian novelist, has to say about routine.

> *"If you think adventure is dangerous, try routine; it is lethal."*
> Paulo Coelho

Slow atrophy is no future for anyone pursuing excellence. Seek variety. Be inquisitive. Be industrious. Aim for top quality. Think hard. Experiment. Learn. Refine your approach.

Neophilia is the desire to experience new things. Research has shown that it is a precursor to a healthier and happier life, because by experiencing something new, our brain is stimulated and we receive a hit of dopamine, creating a rush of excitement.

As humans, we are naturally curious creatures, and by indulging in the new we are creating fresh neural pathways in our brains, allowing us to handle any novel situation. What curiosity could you explore?

Consider this
- Are you fixed in a set routine?
- Are you just doing the same old thing?
- Can you shake things up?

Inspired by *The Excellence Book*

ATTITUDE

ACTION

CREATIVITY

COMMUNICATION

EFFICIENCY

EMPATHY

STRATEGY

SUSTAINABILITY

2. ACTION

> *"The problem with doing nothing is not knowing when you are finished."*
> Nelson DeMille

You can talk as much as you like, but little of it matters unless you actually do something.

We start by explaining how to beat interruptions so that you can get on with what you know needs to be done.

We then discuss different ways to do this, including being a possibilist and an essentialist – seeing opportunity, taking it, and doing precisely what really matters.

But there's no point in forcing something that won't work. To take effective action you need a clear system, so we look at some of those before moving on to dealing with procrastination and waning enthusiasm.

We finish off with how to make effective habits a way of life that can fundamentally change your perspective.

I remove distractions and interference to improve my concentration levels. > BEATING INTERRUPTIONS	2.1
I look at what is possible rather than wild, impractical ideas. > BE A POSSIBILIST	2.2
I am able to prioritise tasks and concentrate on what is truly essential. > BE AN ESSENTIALIST	2.3
I can abandon an idea if it doesn't fit the task properly. > DON'T FORCE FIT	2.4
I prefer acting to just talking about things. > YOU ARE WHAT YOU DO	2.5
I am good at distinguishing between high and low priority projects. > THE THREE BUCKETS	2.6
I consistently meet my deadlines. > BEATING PROCRASTINATION	2.7
I am good at ensuring momentum on initiatives once they are started. > AVOID FIZZLE OUT	2.8
I am good at admitting when approaches are not working. > CHANGING YOUR HABITS	2.9
I thoughtfully consider a wide range of options before deciding on a course of action. > STAND BACK AND TAKE A CLOSER LOOK	2.10

ATTITUDE

ACTION

CREATIVITY

COMMUNICATION

EFFICIENCY

EMPATHY

STRATEGY

SUSTAINABILITY

2.1 BEATING INTERRUPTIONS

I remove distractions and interference to improve my concentration levels.

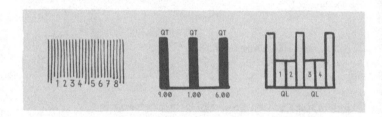

Being interrupted is the bane of anyone's work life. This is particularly true when working in an open plan office. When you walk up the corridor, chances are you will be accosted by someone asking, "Have you got a minute?" Even if you are at your desk and clearly right in the middle of something, you will still be harassed. This kind of persistently interrupted day ends up looking like the barcode on a product.

That's a barcode day, and you can't get a run of time to get anything decent done. It's just too bitty. So, the knack is to divide up time into suitable chunks, distinguishing between two types of work: quantitative and qualitative. Quantitative (QT) work can neither be done well nor badly – it's just stuff that needs to be churned through. Qualitative (QL) work requires more time and absolutely needs to be of high quality.

So now you can plan your day or week in a new way based on the quantitative versus qualitative distinction. Start by allocating short bursts of quantitative time, in which you will knock over a lot of small tasks in one burst. Try not to do this more than three times a day, and never for longer than 30 minutes per session.

Then map out decent runs of time, usually a minimum of an hour, to do some proper thinking or creating. Interlock them with the quantitative bursts, and don't mix the two types of work up. Review this blend based on your personal style, depending on whether you are a morning or evening person. Then apply it to a whole week or even a month.

Consider this
- Do you distinguish between quantitative and qualitative tasks?
- Can you divide up the day by quantitative and qualitative tasks?
- Do you mix up quantitative and qualitative work?

Inspired by *The Intelligent Work Book*

ATTITUDE

ACTION

CREATIVITY

COMMUNICATION

EFFICIENCY

EMPATHY

STRATEGY

SUSTAINABILITY

2.2 BE A POSSIBILIST

I look at what is possible rather than wild, impractical ideas.

Pessimists look smart because they see problems everywhere. They even like it when things go wrong because it proves they were right to be pessimistic. Optimists can often look stupid because they think everything can be done. It is easy for cynics to laugh at their apparently blind enthusiasm.

Possibilists can strike a balance between the two. What's the best possible thing we could do here?

Spiritual bypassing is a "tendency to use spiritual ideas and practices to sidestep or avoid facing unresolved emotional issues, psychological wounds, and unfinished developmental tasks." The term was introduced in the mid-1980s by John Welwood, a Buddhist teacher and psychotherapist. As individuals, we can't be optimistic all the time. If we are continuously positive and, therefore, ignore reality (which includes the bad parts), we are suppressing important parts of ourselves that are there for a reason. Fear and worry are designed to protect us.

Possibilists believe they can find an intelligent way through – staying positive while remaining pragmatic. Most things work out fine, so let's start by assuming that they will. Are you using too much positivity and optimism to avoid difficult situations?

Consider this
- Are you a pessimist?
- Are you an optimist?
- Could you become a possibilist?

Inspired by *The Excellence Book*

ATTITUDE

ACTION

CREATIVITY

COMMUNICATION

EFFICIENCY

EMPATHY

STRATEGY

SUSTAINABILITY

BE AN ESSENTIALIST

I am able to prioritise tasks and concentrate on what is truly essential.

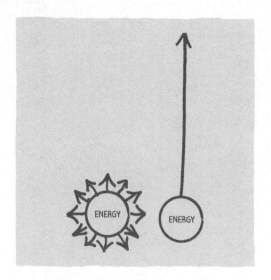

In his book, *Essentialism*, Greg McKeown espouses the disciplined pursuit of less. The nonessentialist is all things to all people, pursues everything in an undisciplined way, and lives a life that does not satisfy. They think that almost everything is essential. The essentialist does less but does it better, creating a life that really matters. They think that almost everything is nonessential. If it isn't a clear yes, then it's a clear no.

Instead of doing many things half-heartedly, do one or two things properly. It takes the same amount of energy but is much more fulfilling. Concentrate only on what is essential.

This concept works just as well for the things that we own. James Wallman's book, *Stuffocation*, explores how we are 'stuffocating' with all the things we have. It's not stuff that makes us happy – it's memories and experiences.

Clutter in the home is clutter in the mind. Marie Kondo's technique asks this question of every item: does it bring you joy, or does it have a practical use? If it doesn't do either, it needs to go. So ask yourself whether you can declutter your life by recycling or giving away things that you no longer need.

Essentialism can become a way of life. If it's not a clear yes, it's a clear no.

Consider this
- Is your working day a mess?
- Could you become an essentialist?
- Can you say no to requests?

Inspired by *The Excellence Book*

ATTITUDE

ACTION

CREATIVITY

COMMUNICATION

EFFICIENCY

EMPATHY

STRATEGY

SUSTAINABILITY

2.4 DON'T FORCE FIT

I can abandon an idea if it doesn't fit the task properly.

Jerry Seinfeld, the American comedian, actor and director, made this wry observation.

> "It's amazing that the amount of news that happens in the world every day always just exactly fits the newspaper."
> Jerry Seinfeld

And of course, it doesn't. And yet, we often hang on to rigid and inflexible constructs to organise what we see and do. You don't chop the legs off a rabbit to fit it in the hutch. So, you don't always have to force fit things into a set format or template.

It can feel counterintuitive, because we are hardwired to find shape where, often, there is none. Like seeing shapes in clouds. Or believing a mass of data has some kind of pattern. Sometimes it just doesn't. And no structured approach can help with that.

Despite the fact that we are pattern-seeking animals, we have to allow for the grey areas in life, and find comfort in them. Black-and-white thinking is a psychological construct whereby if you aren't everything, it means that you are nothing. If you haven't succeeded, then you have failed. If you aren't a brilliant swimmer, it means you must be an awful one. It doesn't allow for any other variations to sit in between.

This thinking only allows for extremes, can leave us feeling inadequate, and is hard to negotiate. Consider whether you fall into the category of a black-and-white thinker and how you can change that approach. Don't force fit what you do into a construct that won't do the job.

Consider this
- Do you always want to find a pattern?
- Can you be flexible?
- Can you tolerate randomness?

Inspired by *The Excellence Book*

ATTITUDE
ACTION
CREATIVITY
COMMUNICATION
EFFICIENCY
EMPATHY
STRATEGY
SUSTAINABILITY

2.5 YOU ARE WHAT YOU DO

I prefer acting to just talking about things.

There is no point in claiming to have a certain attitude when your actions either fail to prove it or, worse, contradict it. Aristotle observed this a long time ago.

> *"We are what we repeatedly do."*
> Aristotle

Thinking is one thing. Doing is quite another. Gina Miller, the businesswoman who initiated a court case against the British government challenging its authority to implement Brexit, said, "What's the point in having a conscience if you never use it?"

The popular blogger and author Mark Manson points this out in his unsubtly named book, *The Subtle Art of Not Giving a F*ck*: "Who you are is defined by what you're willing to struggle for."

You can rarely think your way into a new way of acting. You need to act your way into a new way of thinking. In other words, the action proves the thought. Without action, it merely remains a concept and, as such, doesn't technically exist.

We know that we are happier, more productive human beings if we are working in line with our values. When things at work get tough, which inevitably happens, we know at the very least that we aren't battling with our personal principles.

Company and personal values have become increasingly important over the decades. What values do you live by, and how well do these align with what you do?

Consider this
- Can you align action with attitude?
- Can you act your way into a new way of thinking?
- Do you align company and personal values?

Inspired by *The Excellence Book*

ATTITUDE
ACTION
CREATIVITY
COMMUNICATION
EFFICIENCY
EMPATHY
STRATEGY
SUSTAINABILITY

2.6 THE THREE BUCKETS

I am good at distinguishing between high and low priority projects.

The Three Buckets exercise was introduced by Adam Morgan in his book, *The Pirate Inside*, in 2004. It is an extremely helpful way to categorise projects and work out how effective they are likely to be. Each project must be placed in one of the three buckets.

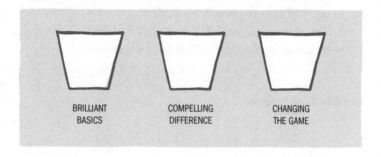

BRILLIANT
BASICS

COMPELLING
DIFFERENCE

CHANGING
THE GAME

On the left is Brilliant Basics. These represent "excellence as standard." You or your company should be doing these well as a matter of course, just like your competitors. In the middle is Compelling Difference. These should be "significantly better than normal." These are demonstrably better than those of your competitors, but not genuinely remarkable. On the right is

Changing The Game. These are "truly extraordinary." They are utterly unique in the market, and genuinely remarkable.

This exercise will reveal whether a sufficient proportion of the projects are going to make a genuine difference. Take a list of all your existing projects. Scrutinise them by the three sets of criteria and place them in the relevant bucket. Look at the quantity in each. Review whether the balance is right. Use the findings to cancel unnecessary projects or search for more enterprising ones.

Consider this
- Can you classify your work in these three ways?
- Can you reduce the number of brilliant basics?
- Can you increase those projects with more merit and potential?

Inspired by *The Diagrams Book*

2.7 BEATING PROCRASTINATION

I consistently meet my deadlines.

Most students put everything off until the last minute. This type
of procrastination almost always leads to a classic essay crisis.
Interestingly, company executives usually do exactly the same thing, so
the pattern of work in most modern businesses is endlessly pressurised.

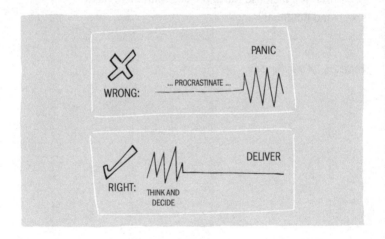

This last-minute approach leads to rushed and usually substandard work. Instead, businesses should do the hard thinking upfront, and so create the conditions for a smooth run to execution or a launch deadline. Most people agree with the principle of this, but protest that there is so much work coming in that they can't keep on top of it all. There are three main strategies that can break this cycle.

1. *Upfront thinking built in.* Make it mandatory company policy to do proper thinking before all major projects or work cycles, whether annually, quarterly, monthly or even weekly.
2. *Think, then delegate.* As long as the right minds have thought properly at the beginning, then technical specialists and executors can get on and do the work once direction is set.
3. *Anticipate logjams.* A pragmatic overview of any run of work can usually predict when the trouble will occur. Doing this at the beginning and taking appropriate steps will reduce their severity or predict whether they will happen at all.

Consider this
- Do you suffer from the essay crisis problem?
- Can you anticipate logjams?
- Can you stop leaving things to the last minute?

Inspired by *The Intelligent Work Book*

ATTITUDE

ACTION

CREATIVITY

COMMUNICATION

EFFICIENCY

EMPATHY

STRATEGY

SUSTAINABILITY

2.8 AVOID FIZZLE OUT

I am good at ensuring momentum on initiatives once they are started.

Almost every initiative or project in the world loses momentum at some point. It's human nature. We are very excited at the beginning and the enthusiasm drops off. This can be described as a motivational dip. The interesting thing is that this phenomenon can almost always be predicted.

So, there is no point in pretending that it won't happen. It is far more intelligent and effective to anticipate the fizzle out and build fail-safes into the plan from the start. Check-ins, reminders, incentives and sometimes even a quiet talking to all play their part in keeping the plan on track. Be realistic about human motivation and get practical.

Once important decisions are made, commitment needs to run through the entire organisation. Without robust and effective internal communication, principles can easily weaken in the face of day-to-day reality, as the graphic, adapted from *Brand Manners* by Pringle and Gordon, nicely illustrates. This disconnect is often described as a strategy/execution gap.

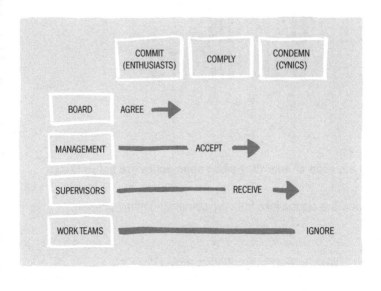

Board-level enthusiasm means little if initiatives are met with cynicism on the front line. Strategies need to be fully explained to be successfully embraced at all levels of the business. If you are supervising a project, anticipate this and put measures in place to keep momentum going.

Consider this
- Do you assume that people will do what they are told?
- Can you deal with resistance to action?
- Can you anticipate fizzle out?

Inspired by *The Sustainable Business Book*

ATTITUDE

ACTION

CREATIVITY

COMMUNICATION

EFFICIENCY

EMPATHY

STRATEGY

SUSTAINABILITY

2.9 CHANGING YOUR HABITS

I am good at admitting when approaches are not working.

Here's a classic joke from the comedian Tommy Cooper.

> I said to the doctor: "It hurts when I do this."
>
> Tommy raises his arm.
>
> He said, "Well, don't do it then."

The logic is irrefutable. If something doesn't work, or you don't like doing it, then don't do it. Most people are perfectly intelligent. And yet they often keep doing the same things again and again without any noticeable improvement in the outcome.

Smart decisions involve identifying what fails to work and systematically removing those defunct activities. So if things aren't working, stop doing them. Decide not to carry on. Think of something better and do that instead.

Aparigraha is the concept of nonattachment in yogic teachings. It teaches that we must learn not to cling to possessions and identities because it prevents us from moving freely and accepting the reality that life will change. Our identities and material possessions shift. If we attach ourselves to them, it makes these changes a lot harder to stomach.

We will keep circling within who we think we should be, and what we think we should own, to live up to some sort of expectation. But if we learn to release ourselves from these attachments, and accept the ebbs and flows that life brings, we will be much happier. What possessions, habits or identities are you attached to?

Consider this
- Do you often go round in circles?
- Can you stop doing the same thing again and again?
- Can you change your habits to get a better result?

Inspired by *The Excellence Book*

ATTITUDE

ACTION

CREATIVITY

COMMUNICATION

EFFICIENCY

EMPATHY

STRATEGY

SUSTAINABILITY

2.10 STAND BACK AND TAKE A CLOSER LOOK

I thoughtfully consider a wide range of options before deciding on a course of action.

If you are going to be strategically decisive, then you need to widen your options, reality-test your assumptions, attain distance before deciding, and prepare to be wrong. That's the advice of experts Chip and Dan Heath.

Stage 1. Avoid a narrow time frame, multitrack (consider more than one option simultaneously), and find someone who has already solved your problem. Give yourself time, look at lots of possibilities and take wide-ranging advice.

Stage 2. Consider doing the opposite, zoom in and out between the big picture and the detail. Try *ooching* – a Southern US word for running small experiments to test theories.

Stage 3. Overcome short-term emotion and honour your core priorities. Pragmatic, fact-based thinking works, not so-called gut feel.

ATTITUDE

ACTION

CREATIVITY

COMMUNICATION

EFFICIENCY

EMPATHY

STRATEGY

SUSTAINABILITY

> *Stage 4.* Bookend the future by mapping out a range of outcomes from very bad to very good and then set up tripwires to provide sufficient early warning of adjustments needed later.

All of this takes time, so you need to consider your actions in a wider context. Consider the widest range of possibilities. Test the effectiveness of your chosen action with a quick pilot, then take the emotion out of it and prepare to be wrong. If you are wrong, then you may have to try a different approach until you get it right.

Beware of overly heavy emotional commitment too early in the process. If you are set on a direction before you have the evidence, then it is much harder to change your mind later on.

Consider this
- Can you widen your options and attain distance?
- Can you stand back and take a closer look?
- Can you pause to gain perspective?

Inspired by *The Smart Strategy Book*

3. CREATIVITY

> *"I can't understand why people are frightened of new ideas.*
> *I'm frightened of the old ones."*
> John Cage

Coming up with ideas is easy for some and hard for others, but there is a discipline to it.

We start by explaining why creativity needs to be married to commercial thinking from the outset and how important it is to get the brief realistic and clear before generating ideas.

We move on to how to use your subconscious and some clever techniques before making decisions about which ideas to progress.

You need to allow ideas to flourish before running final checks on whether to proceed with them.

We finish off with how to give your ideas the widest possible chance of being well received.

I am able to combine commercial realism with the creative process from the start. > THE CREATIVITY AND COMMERCE CROSSROADS	3.1	ATTITUDE
I always make sure that the objective or brief is clear before idea generation begins. > THE BRIEFING STAR	3.2	ACTION
I always assess the true complexity of a creative challenge before generating ideas. > THREE GOOD, THREE BAD	3.3	CREATIVITY
I trust my mind to arrive at intelligent solutions eventually. > TRAINING YOUR DEPTH MIND	3.4	COMMUNICATION
I look beyond the category in which I operate to inspire new ideas. > CATEGORY STEALING	3.5	EFFICIENCY
I am prepared to drop ideas and projects that aren't showing sufficient progress. > ENSURING HIGH QUALITY IDEAS	3.6	EMPATHY
I am good at reducing a large number of ideas down to a manageable number. > ESTABLISHING POTENTIAL	3.7	STRATEGY
I allow ideas to develop and flourish before killing them off too quickly. > LETTING IDEAS FLOURISH	3.8	SUSTAINABILITY
I have a good track record of predicting ideas that will be successful. > THE PREMORTEM	3.9	
I am able to generate inspiring ideas that people get excited about. > GIVE IT SOCIAL CURRENCY	3.10	

3.1 THE CREATIVITY AND COMMERCE CROSSROADS

I am able to combine commercial realism with the creative process from the start.

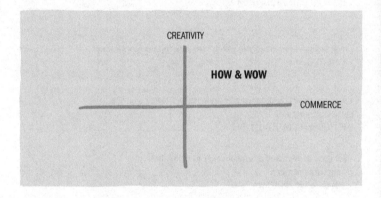

Innovation must build ideas at the crossroads of creativity and commerce, according to Mark Payne, founder of the innovation company Fahrenheit 212. The failure rates of most innovations are absurdly high, culminating in unicorns – visions that are lovely to think about, but only doable and profitable in some imaginary world.

What is needed is a *Money and Magic* approach, sometimes called *how and wow*. That's where the ideas people and the commercial people work together from the start to solve both a big customer problem and a big business problem in one bold move.

By the midpoint in their development, nearly all ideas solve a customer need. But they should only be implemented if they also solve a business need for the company.

The moral is: don't suspend commercial questions too early in the process. This two-sided thinking (customer need and company need) must be present from day one, because the best results appear at the crossroads of these two requirements.

Don't buy into the myth that creativity is most effective when it's unencumbered by practical imperatives. It's not true. So having random ideas without understanding the real commercial issues doesn't get you anywhere. For a truly effective approach, get the practical people working at the beginning with the ideas people. This will save you generating scores of idealistic concepts that can't be executed.

Consider this
- Can you combine creativity and commerce?
- Do you pursue money as a goal in its own right?
- Do you pursue ideas without working out if they are viable?

Inspired by *The Smart Strategy Book*

ATTITUDE

ACTION

CREATIVITY

COMMUNICATION

EFFICIENCY

EMPATHY

STRATEGY

SUSTAINABILITY

3.2 THE BRIEFING STAR

I always make sure that the objective or brief is clear before idea generation begins.

The best briefs are clinically simple. If you are running an ideas session, or simply setting yourself a task, you should restrict yourself to one sentence. This is worth spending a lot of time on, because if it is not clear, no decent response will be forthcoming. To get an immediate fix on what you need to do, use The Briefing Star.

Start with what. What are we trying to achieve? Then confirm the sense of that by asking why? Why are we trying to do this? If the answers are too vague or unsatisfactory, then change the what, or scrap the project altogether.

Then describe the who? Who is this aimed at? The brief can now be expressed as a statement *(Our objective is to revolutionise the X category)*, or a question *(How do we double the size of Brand X?)* If the thinking is sufficiently clear and robust, it may be acceptable to have both an objective and a question: *Our objective is to revolutionise the X category. What single product feature would achieve this?*

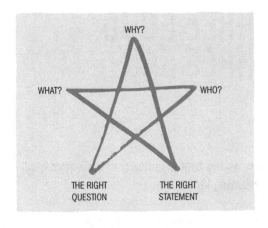

WHY?

WHAT?   WHO?

THE RIGHT   THE RIGHT
QUESTION   STATEMENT

ATTITUDE

ACTION

CREATIVITY

COMMUNICATION

EFFICIENCY

EMPATHY

STRATEGY

SUSTAINABILITY

You might want to try this exercise. Choose a business issue that needs serious attention. Spend time articulating it in as short and clear way as possible. First ask, what are we trying to achieve? Do not proceed until this is absolutely clear. If needed, ask the why question to cross-check whether the what is sufficiently robust. Add the why. Experiment with using a statement as the brief or question, or both in tandem. Leave the result and come back to it later, make changes if necessary, then check with a respected colleague to see if they think it is a decent brief.

Consider this
- Do you always make sure that the brief is clear?
- Are you always clear what you are doing?
- Are you always clear about who it is aimed at?

Inspired by *The Ideas Book*

3.3 THREE GOOD, THREE BAD

I always assess the true complexity of a creative challenge before generating ideas.

Many idea sessions are derailed by negative material and attitude. It only takes one moaner and the whole thing can veer off in an unwanted direction. If you believe this is a possibility, then the *Three Good Three Bad* technique is excellent for combating it.

Instead of allowing negative comments to creep into proceedings, the technique deliberately seeks out the bad stuff, deals with it early, and offsets it with good stuff. This is sometimes called the car park – a place where all the negativity is parked.

GOOD		BAD	
1	_____	1	_____
2	_____	2	_____
3	_____	3	_____

All attendees are asked to write down three bad things about the product/project/brief, and then three good things. This draws the sting out of all negative comments. They are not forced to generate three of each, but three is the maximum. The results are reviewed and summarised by the facilitator. Usually there is a significant overlap, and there is much to be learned about the degree of consensus, or an absolute focus on just one deficiency. It also shows how much the attendees really know about the subject.

The exercise should always be done first, and should never last more than one hour, or 20% of the meeting time. All the good features are then used as inspiration to go on to provide an excellent solution.

As an exercise, think hard to work out if there appears to be an insurmountable problem with the brief: an unsatisfactory history to the project, a nasty constraint, or simply a prevailing culture of defeatism or cynicism. Use the technique to flush these issues out early and turn them into positive action.

Consider this
- Do you get the bad stuff out from the beginning?
- Can you identify the good stuff?
- Can you form a realistic basis for tasks and projects?

Inspired by *The Ideas Book*

ATTITUDE

ACTION

CREATIVITY

COMMUNICATION

EFFICIENCY

EMPATHY

STRATEGY

SUSTAINABILITY

3.4 TRAINING YOUR DEPTH MIND

I trust my mind to arrive at intelligent solutions eventually.

Making better use of your Depth Mind is an important skill for creative thinkers. Your Depth Mind is your subconscious. Once you have experienced an *unconcealing* (the first instinct of an issue that needs a solution), then you can start to trust your Depth Mind to sort things out and generate solutions once you have 'briefed' it.

But this doesn't just happen automatically. You need to train your Depth Mind and you can do that in various ways.

1. Be constantly curious.
2. Practice serendipity (the more you think, the more it appears you are in 'the right place at the right time').
3. Become a Mental Magpie (collect stimuli often and from odd places).
4. Widen your span of relevance (many inventions were conceived by those working in other fields and, as the saying goes, chance favours the prepared mind).

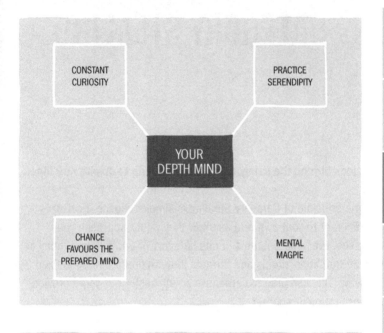

ATTITUDE

ACTION

CREATIVITY

COMMUNICATION

EFFICIENCY

EMPATHY

STRATEGY

SUSTAINABILITY

Consider this

- Do you brief your depth mind?
- Are you a mental magpie?
- Do you prepare your mind to take advantage of chance?

Inspired by *The Ideas Book*

3.5 CATEGORY STEALING

I look beyond the category in which I operate to inspire new ideas.

The principle of Category Stealing is simple: choose a category different to your own and ask how they would approach your issue. Everyone operates in one category or another, and many of the traditions, rituals and formats in them operate in quite fixed ways. This can lead to sameness in one sector but could provide inspiration in another.

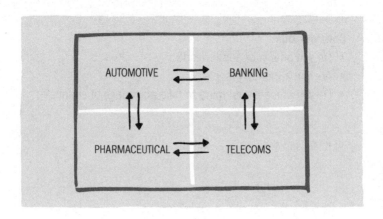

Start by listing a number of other categories. If you need reminding, scan the share prices in a newspaper, search online or watch the TV for an evening. You will soon have an A–Z of categories. Identify the characteristics of well-defined ones, such as their usual approach to finance, branding, distribution, price, product features and so on.

Then work out what you can steal to apply to your brief. If a whole category doesn't have clearly defined traits, then take one brand that does. For example, how would Apple or Coca-Cola do this? If you work in a fairly obscure category, then look to the wisdom of well-known ones. If you work in a well-understood one, take the time to investigate more unusual ones. There is always something to learn.

Choose three or four categories that are far removed from your own. Work out their main features and processes. Home in on one brand in the category that is a particular success if necessary. Now imagine using that approach to grapple with your brief. Repeat for various categories as required.

Consider this
- Do you look to categories other than your own?
- Can you consider how they would approach your challenge?
- Can you apply that thinking to your category?

Inspired by *The Ideas Book*

ATTITUDE

ACTION

CREATIVITY

COMMUNICATION

EFFICIENCY

EMPATHY

STRATEGY

SUSTAINABILITY

3.6 ENSURING HIGH QUALITY IDEAS

I am prepared to drop ideas and projects that aren't showing sufficient progress.

A good way to improve quality in creative idea generation is to understand the potential barriers that may prevent ideas from becoming reality. Each notch on the line between failure and success represents a barrier to action, in this case a series of reasons the idea will never get off the ground. These could be practical, financial or personal.

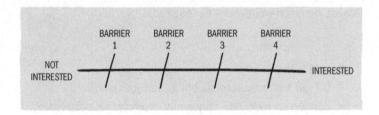

Bear in mind that the personal barriers could be the most powerful in any company – perhaps a senior executive or committee that has the ability to block the idea. By mapping the decision-making process diagrammatically, each barrier to enactment can be identified and isolated.

A plan to knock each one down can then be devised, or if the conclusion is that the idea will never be approved because there are too many barriers, it can be abandoned.

Choose an idea that you believe has merit. Use the axis to plot all the reasons that the company or executives in influential positions might have for not proceeding with it. If relevant, put the barriers in chronological order, or place the biggest or hardest ones first, to the far left. Then come up with a plan to knock down each barrier. If a barrier cannot be removed, you may have to admit defeat.

Consider this
- Can you work out what is not likely to happen?
- Can you identify the barriers to success?
- Can you work out how to overcome them?

Inspired by *The Ideas Book*

3.7 ESTABLISHING POTENTIAL

I am good at reducing a large number of ideas down to a manageable number.

The Potential Pyramid is very useful for grouping a large number of ideas into broad groups to get an initial feel for volume and potential. You can choose your own language, but for the purposes of this construct, we will use promising, possible and poor.

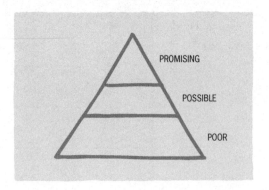

Promising means that everyone agrees the idea has potential, albeit the details are unlikely to be clear yet. This doesn't matter. Possible means there are some reservations, but the view is that further investigation to prove/disprove potential would nevertheless be time well spent. Poor means there is significant doubt about whether to bother with progressing it. Many ideas seem great when first generated but, on reflection, they don't hold up under scrutiny.

Write the number of ideas in each layer. If there is just one in the promising layer, this may be enough. If there are none, then look to the possible layer and be more specific about what to spend more time on. If there is enough potential in either of those, then drop everything in the bottom layer.

When you have generated all your ideas, spread them all out on a table. What is the total number? How many of each in the three categories? If there are no promising ones, look to the possible section. If there is enough potential in both top layers, discard all the rest and concentrate resource in the right place.

Consider this
- Can you distinguish between promising, possible and poor ideas?
- Are you brutal on the weaker ideas?
- Do you throw out the OK in favour of better ideas?

Inspired by *The Ideas Book*

ATTITUDE

ACTION

CREATIVITY

COMMUNICATION

EFFICIENCY

EMPATHY

STRATEGY

SUSTAINABILITY

3.8 LETTING IDEAS FLOURISH

I allow ideas to develop and flourish before killing them off too quickly.

Here we look at a technique that attends to two sides of the same issue.

1. Allow an idea to flourish properly.
2. Prevent it from being chipped away at before it has even got off the ground.

Many companies and individuals have more creativity than they realise, but they inadvertently stifle it or channel it in the wrong directions. There is a time and place for judging ideas but, in the embryonic phase, ideas should not be diluted until their full potential has been investigated. So, to avoid death by a thousand cuts, subject the idea to four examinations.

1. Trust your instinct: do you like it?
2. Leave it alone: do not be tempted to fiddle with it.
3. Overcommit: how could you devote every possible resource to it?
4. Sacrifice: what would you be prepared to sacrifice to make it happen?

ATTITUDE

ACTION

CREATIVITY

COMMUNICATION

EFFICIENCY

EMPATHY

STRATEGY

SUSTAINABILITY

TRUST YOUR INSTINCT	LEAVE IT ALONE
OVERCOMMIT	SACRIFICE

These last two come from Adam Morgan in his book, *Eating the Big Fish*. Pull together the best ideas you have so far. Subject them to the four-stage process, each idea in turn. If you suspect that any of the ideas have already been watered down, then go back to their original source and examine their unadulterated form. If necessary, reconvene the group to scrutinise the idea anew.

Consider this
- Do you accept that ideas are fragile?
- Do you dismiss ideas too quickly?
- Can you let them develop properly before rejecting them?

Inspired by *The Ideas Book*

3.9 THE PREMORTEM

I have a good track record of predicting ideas that will be successful.

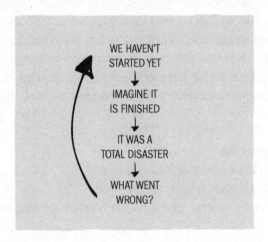

WE HAVEN'T
STARTED YET
↓
IMAGINE IT
IS FINISHED
↓
IT WAS A
TOTAL DISASTER
↓
WHAT WENT
WRONG?

The Premortem is a great way to run a final check to judge whether an idea is sufficiently worthy to proceed with. It was invented by Gary Klein and summarised by Daniel Kahneman in his book, *Thinking, Fast and Slow.*

The procedure is simple: when a team or an organisation has almost come to an important decision but has not formally committed itself, the decision-makers gather for a brief session. They are asked to imagine that it is one year later, and that the idea has been a complete disaster. They then have to write a short history of what happened.

Of course, it is important that such a review is conducted long enough before it is too late and everyone is totally committed to proceeding. The Premortem could prevent many a disaster. By contrast, a postmortem may be useless.

To put this all into practice, follow these steps. Articulate the idea. Draw up a list of the decision makers. Gather them for a short meeting. Ask them to imagine that it is one year in the future. Everything went ahead, but it was a disaster. Get them to write a short synopsis of what went wrong. Examine the results to see if the group has revealed a fatal flaw in the idea.

Consider this
- Before committing, do you work out what could go wrong?
- Can you imagine the worst and fix what is necessary?
- Can you abandon a project if a flaw is revealed?

Inspired by *The Ideas Book*

ATTITUDE

ACTION

CREATIVITY

COMMUNICATION

EFFICIENCY

EMPATHY

STRATEGY

SUSTAINABILITY

3.10 GIVE IT SOCIAL CURRENCY

I am able to generate inspiring ideas that people get excited about.

Once you have alighted on an idea, how will you get your audience to understand it and like it? Your message is more likely to catch on if you give it what author Jonah Berger calls *social currency*. Make it contagious. This requires:

Social Currency: make people look intelligent if they pass it on. We share things that make us look good. Can you find something that makes people feel like insiders?

Triggers: provide related stimuli to remind people to talk about it. Top of mind leads to tip of tongue. What cues can make people think about your product or idea?

Emotion: when we care, we share. Ideas need to make people feel something. Concentrate on feelings: how can you kindle the fire and get people talking about it?

Public: we need to see other people joining in. If it's built to show, it's built to grow. Can people see others using your product, or evidence that sticks around when they have?

Practical Value: it needs to be useful – news you can use. Does the subject matter help people help others?

Stories: increase appeal and help engage people. Information often travels under the guise of idle chatter. Is your product part of a broader story that people want to share?

Follow these components and your idea is more likely to find favour with people, go viral or lead to social transmission. Of course, just because you follow some appropriate steps, it doesn't mean that everyone is going to love what you communicate. But you can work out the sequence in advance, anticipate the sticking points and build your approach appropriately.

Consider this
- Can you make an idea capture peoples' imagination?
- Can you create triggers and make people look good?
- Can you create messages that people care about?

Inspired by *The Smart Strategy Book*

ATTITUDE

ACTION

CREATIVITY

COMMUNICATION

EFFICIENCY

EMPATHY

STRATEGY

SUSTAINABILITY

4. COMMUNICATION

> "The void created by the failure to communicate is soon filled with poison, drivel and misrepresentation."
> C. Northcote Parkinson

There is no form of communication that cannot be misunderstood.

We start by explaining why it is critical to have a point of view and a clear line of argument from the start.

We move on to looking at the power of sequence and pacing, and why brevity and the removal of bull is essential to clear communication.

In order to communicate effectively, you need to listen intently and then establish a constructive consensus.

We finish off with why it doesn't pay to overthink things and how to learn from your mistakes.

I don't embark on presentations until I have a clear point of view and a persuasive line of argument. > FROM POV TO LOA	4.1
My formal presentations are clear and concise. > THE POWER OF SEQUENCE	4.2
I use a mix of visual and verbal methods to accommodate a broad range of audiences. > THE WHITTLING WEDGE	4.3
My written communications are always as short and concise as possible. > SAY LESS FOR MORE IMPACT	4.4
I avoid cliché and corporate jargon. > BANISHING BULL	4.5
I always make sure that something has been achieved before making claims. > DO THINGS, THEN TELL PEOPLE	4.6
I believe that listening is a vital element of successful communication. > IS ANYONE REALLY LISTENING?	4.7
I am good at the art of negotiation. > HOW TO NEGOTIATE	4.8
I think things through clearly, but don't overthink them. > DON'T OVERTHINK	4.9
In the event of any miscommunication, I learn from my mistakes. > LEARNING FROM MISTAKES	4.10

ATTITUDE

ACTION

CREATIVITY

COMMUNICATION

EFFICIENCY

EMPATHY

STRATEGY

SUSTAINABILITY

4.1 FROM POV TO LOA

I don't embark on presentations until I have a clear point of view and a persuasive line of argument.

You can't start writing a presentation until you have a point of view (POV). If you don't have one, look at the Creativity section. Once you do, you need to map out your Line of Argument (LOA). Follow these ten steps.

1. **Killer Title Goes Here.** Don't waste the chance with a bland one.
2. **Start with a Bang.** Use a grabber to grab their attention.
3. **Make Assertions and Back Them Up.** See next.
4. **Tell the Story of Your Strategic Journey.** Don't just dive into the answer.
5. **Tell Them the Central Idea.** Clearly and simply.
6. **In the Context of ...** Show that you understand the broader picture.
7. **Tone of Voice.** Change it if necessary to relate to your audience.
8. **Products and Processes.** Only mention these at the end, not the beginning.
9. **The Programme.** Map it out as simply as possible.
10. **The Appendix.** Put everything that ruins the line of argument in here.

The knack with the middle section is to provide an intelligent interplay between assertions and facts. Assertions on their own, without backup, can be dismissed or simply disagreed with by the audience. Facts on their own are dull, and don't get you anywhere without a point of view. The ideal blend is a series of assertions (A) coupled to facts (F) or, if you prefer, a series of facts linked to your point of view (POV) on what to do as a result.

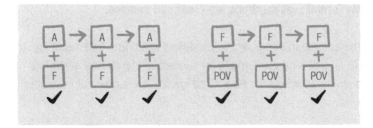

The presentation requires a broad-ranging beginning, a logical argument in the middle and a clear recommendation at the end (see 4.3).

Consider this
- Can you establish your POV?
- Can you design a coherent LOA?
- Can you avoid assertions without facts or vice versa?

Inspired by *The Intelligent Work Book*

ATTITUDE

ACTION

CREATIVITY

COMMUNICATION

EFFICIENCY

EMPATHY

STRATEGY

SUSTAINABILITY

4.2 THE POWER OF SEQUENCE

My formal presentations are clear and concise.

The animation company Pixar, creators of *Finding Nemo* and *Toy Story*, has a proven formula for successful storytelling. What has become known as the Pixar Pitch involves six sequential sentences:

Once upon a time, A.

Every day, B.

One day, C.

Because of that, D.

Because of that, E.

Until finally, F.

All successful communication blends this kind of appeal with flexibility. Getting the order right is critical for clear explanation. And the power of the sequence ensures that your audience comes along with you.

Concentrate on having a really strong start, a memorable finish, and a tight, cogent middle section. People only remember 20% of what you say in the middle bit, so keep it short.

Make sure you show your workings. Facts on their own are dull, and opinions on their own can be refuted. So the ideal blend is a series of assertions coupled to evidence or, if you prefer, a series of facts linked to your point of view on what to do as a result.

Consider this
- Do you believe that the order in which you say things matters?
- Can you create a coherent, cogent presentation?
- Could you use the Pixar Pitch?

Inspired by *The Smart Thinking Book*

ATTITUDE

ACTION

CREATIVITY

COMMUNICATION

EFFICIENCY

EMPATHY

STRATEGY

SUSTAINABILITY

4.3 THE WHITTLING WEDGE

I use a mix of visual and verbal methods to accommodate a broad range of audiences.

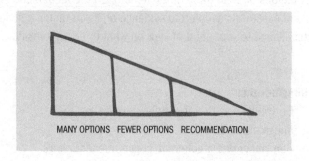

MANY OPTIONS   FEWER OPTIONS   RECOMMENDATION

The Whittling Wedge is brilliant for telling a strategic story and narrowing down options. This allows the presenter to explain their workings, show that a lot was considered, but still end with a clear, preferably single, recommendation. Starting on the left, many options can be introduced, analysed and then systematically rejected, using as much rationale and detail as is appropriate to the subject.

By the middle of the wedge, you should be down to a maximum of three or four possibilities. These can be analysed in even more detail, or even recommended for detailed research.

Finally, the presenter arrives on the right with a beautifully argued recommendation that has covered all considerations.

Overall, whittling the argument in this way emulates how equation questions must be successfully answered in maths exams. You can't just stampede to the answer – you have to show your workings. The more complex the story, the more the audience appreciates this explanatory approach.

Choose a presentation or story that needs explaining, ideally one with quite a few options or wide-ranging subject matter. Use the Whittling Wedge to start broad, and then reduce the number of options or topics systematically. Try to arrive at the end with one clear recommendation or point of view.

Consider this
- Can you map a presentation visually?
- Can you whittle wide-ranging material down to fewer options?
- Can you explain your workings and arrive at a recommendation?

Inspired by *The Diagrams Book*

ATTITUDE

ACTION

CREATIVITY

COMMUNICATION

EFFICIENCY

EMPATHY

STRATEGY

SUSTAINABILITY

4.4 SAY LESS FOR MORE IMPACT

My written communications are always as short and concise as possible.

You can make a bigger impact by saying less. According to Joseph McCormack in his book, *Brief*, most day-to-day communications are unfocused and unclear. In a world where everyone is inundated with too much information and is highly inattentive, being brief isn't a nicety, it's a necessity. People who struggle with brevity suffer variously from any or all of the seven Cs: cowardice, (over)confidence, callousness, comfort, confusion, complication and carelessness. Audiences of all types that are mind-filled rather than mindful suffer from inundation, inattention, interruption and impatience. There are four things you need to do to communicate effectively and efficiently:

> ***Map it:*** map out the argument, then trim volumes of information from it.
>
> ***Tell it:*** use narrative storytelling to explain the message in a clear, concise and compelling way.
>
> ***Talk it:*** turn monologues into productive conversations: **T**alk, **A**ctively **L**isten, **C**onverse.
>
> ***Show it:*** use visuals to attract attention and capture the imagination.

Brevity is not just about shortness. It takes various forms. Light brevity is being concise without comprehension. Deep brevity is being succinct with savvy. Aim for the latter.

Pretty much every business idea is sold to colleagues and bosses in written presentations. These should all be subject to trimming. McCormack identifies three levels of information that can make a persuasive case:

- *Level 1* details are absolutely essential.
- *Level 2* details add a little flavour but shouldn't take up too much time.
- *Level 3* items weigh the story down and don't make it noticeably better.

Always ask: is your presentation or document too long-winded? Long doesn't equal interesting. In fact, it probably means vague and confusing. Do you have too many Level 3 points? Take your presentation, grab some sticky notes and write one strong point only per note – the fewer the better. Then spend a little time putting them in a persuasive order. Remember: if your colleagues don't understand it, then they are unlikely to agree with you.

Consider this
- Can you say just enough and not protest too much?
- Can you distinguish between levels of necessary detail?
- Can you go for deep brevity?

Inspired by *The Smart Strategy Book*

ATTITUDE

ACTION

CREATIVITY

COMMUNICATION

EFFICIENCY

EMPATHY

STRATEGY

SUSTAINABILITY

4.5 BANISHING BULL

I avoid cliché and corporate jargon.

There are many ways to remove bullshit from business communication. Bullshit exchange almost becomes a ritual in many companies – a way of life. According to André Spicer, there are some ways to slow down the exchange of bull:

1. *Reality test:* get the facts on whether something truly works or not, before initiating it.
2. *Rationality test:* poor reasoning is a hallmark of bull. Always ask: why does this need to be done at all?
3. *Meaning test:* do the concepts genuinely make sense to the audience? If not, ditch the project or come up with something better and clearer.
4. *Intentionality test:* what intentions and motives lie behind the bull? Are we deluding ourselves here?
5. *Clarifiability test:* can this thing be clarified and will it definitely help the business?

To communicate better, you need to be more distinctive than everyone else. George Orwell recommended that whenever you are crafting a message, scrupulous writers need to ask these questions of every sentence.

1. *What am I trying to say?* Clear intent from the start.
2. *What words will express it?* Think hard.
3. *What image or idiom will make it clearer?* Is there one?
4. *Is this image fresh enough to have an effect?* If not, think of a better one.
5. *Could I put it more shortly?* Ruthlessly self-edit.
6. *Have I said anything that is avoidably ugly?* If so, improve it.

ATTITUDE

ACTION

CREATIVITY

COMMUNICATION

EFFICIENCY

EMPATHY

STRATEGY

SUSTAINABILITY

Here are six ways to stop rewarding bull:

1. *Limit attention to it:* do not publicise shoddy work.
2. *Don't legitimise it:* don't endorse or approve of it.
3. *Provide alternative bases of self-confidence:* promote clearer expression.
4. *Make stupidity costly:* highlight examples of vague and obscure communication.
5. *Make increasing organisational load costly:* constantly remove layers of bull.
6. *Track trust:* introduce a metric that links clear communication with better understanding, trust and effective results.

Overall, always challenge yourself to find different ways to say things. Look for a wider vocabulary to convey thinking and communication that is more distinctive than that of others.

Consider this
- Do you rail against bull?
- Can you generate clear communication?
- Do you avoid vagueness?

Inspired by *The Bullshit-Free Book*

4.6 DO THINGS, THEN TELL PEOPLE

I always make sure that something has been achieved before making claims.

Larry Weber's book, *Authentic Marketing*, explains the principles of storydoing and datatelling. As the author says, this may sound like marketing speak, but it's really about moving an organisation from telling stories to being an active part of them and providing the proof. This is all about showing what a company is doing to solve important problems for their customers.

As with all such initiatives, it is important to outline measurable objectives that can realistically be accomplished in a specific time period and then track and measure them as progress is made.

Quantifiable data is important to validate this progress and should be included in the narrative. It can be used to create simple and powerful visuals, charts, graphs and marketing claims – all powerful forms of communication when used in the right way. Here are some techniques for creating compelling, continuing stories based on storydoing and datatelling. Ensure the right sequence. Measure progress first. Prove your claim with the data. Only then tell people.

TELL IT VISUALLY	Without a doubt, visual is the best format today. Repurpose stories across multiple visual media for maximum impact.
BE SELECTIVE WITH WORDS	Use words that are vibrant, descriptive, evoke emotions, ignite the senses and draw readers in.
HIGHLIGHT HUMILITY	Bring forth the people in your stories. Share their voices (including employees, customers and suppliers).
LET CREATIVITY SHINE	Make the best use of the technical tools now readily available and tell stories with creativity.
KEEP IT REAL	People will sniff out even the slightest hint of manipulation or marketing speak – so keep it honest and genuine, with a little dose of humility (and no hubris).
ENSURE IT'S ALWAYS ON	Your company's ethical journey will have a beginning and many chapters but should not have an end. It should be living, breathing and evolving.

Consider this
- Do you measure progress so that you can datatell?
- Can you enact the story first?
- Do you act before you tell?

Inspired by *The Ethical Business Book*

ATTITUDE

ACTION

CREATIVITY

COMMUNICATION

EFFICIENCY

EMPATHY

STRATEGY

SUSTAINABILITY

4.7 IS ANYONE REALLY LISTENING?

I believe that listening is a vital element of successful communication.

Listening is a highly underrated skill. The most successful people in business listen more than they speak, so that they fully understand a situation. Note: the words listen and silent share the same letters.

How good are you at listening? Evidence now shows that many people are good at making it look as though they are listening when they are doing nothing of the sort. Everyone should improve their listening skills for better working effectiveness. Have a look at this list of false listening approaches from *The Sales Person's Secret Code*, by Mills, Ridley, Laker and Chapman.

> *Dreaming:* I am often thinking about something else while the other person is talking.
> *Answer Preparing:* during conversations, often I am waiting for a pause, so I can spit out an answer that I'm already preparing.
> *Compulsive/Impulsive:* I often say something without thinking first or to fill a silence.
> *Ambushing:* I often fake listen just so I can get in my comments.

ATTITUDE

ACTION

CREATIVITY

COMMUNICATION

EFFICIENCY

EMPATHY

STRATEGY

SUSTAINABILITY

Judging: I practice selective listening. I hear the things I want to hear based upon my own prejudices.
Not Fully Present: I'm often unaware of the message the person is sending through body language and/or vocal intonation.
Noise-Induced Stress: I often embark on a call or meeting when there is background noise in the environment that hinders my ability to listen.
Comparing: I listen through filters, based on past experiences with other customers/colleagues.

Try not to succumb to any of these approaches, because they are deceptive and sometimes devious. Give people your full attention to create the conditions for excellent two-way communication.

Consider this
- Do you know that many people are not genuinely listening?
- Do you agree that better listening = better communication?
- Can you handle those who are not 'fully present'?

Inspired by *The Ethical Business Book*

4.8 HOW TO NEGOTIATE

I am good at the art of negotiation.

The IF Triangle is a crucial ally in any negotiation because
it covers the only three variables that are ever at stake when
a customer is considering whether to make a purchase.
The three questions are always:

1. Will it do the job? (quality)
2. How much will it cost? (price)
3. When can I have it? (timing)

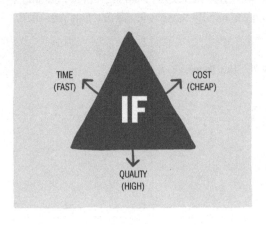

When negotiating, there can always be some flexibility on any two of these variables, but never on all three. For example, the price can usually be reduced if more time is allowed. Quicker delivery may be possible for a premium price. And although no one will ever admit to wanting low quality, things can often be short-circuited.

It is called the IF Triangle because a good way to enact a successful negotiating stance is to start every sentence in the negotiation with the word *If*. It is impossible to finish a sentence that begins with *If* without attaching a condition – a crucial weapon in any successful negotiation. Examples include: *"If I have to deliver it by Friday, the price will have to increase,"* and *"If you need the price reduced, I will need longer to do the job."*

To test all of this, choose an issue that is the subject of negotiation. Write down the time, cost and quality parameters. Devise three sentences beginning with "If..." that define your negotiation stance.

Consider this
- Do you understand the relationship between time, cost and quality?
- Can you resist pressure on too many variables?
- When negotiating, do you use the word 'if'?

Inspired by *The Diagrams Book*

ATTITUDE

ACTION

CREATIVITY

COMMUNICATION

EFFICIENCY

EMPATHY

STRATEGY

SUSTAINABILITY

4.9 DON'T OVERTHINK

I think things through clearly, but don't overthink them.

Here's a joke from American comedian Demetri Martin.

> *"The other day I was thinking, 'I just overthink things.'*
> *And then I thought, 'Do I, though?'"*
> Demetri Martin

That's mental circularity for you. There are times when thinking too much is detrimental. Obsessing over something can be unhealthy, and even counterproductive.

If you overthink something rather than just think clearly about it, you can actually *unthink* it and end up back where you started. Blaise Pascal, the French mathematician, said, "All of man's misery comes from his incapacity to sit alone in an empty, quiet room."

Thoughts usually lead to actions. And actions have consequences. Think, but don't overthink.

Consider this

- Do you think, but not overthink?
- Can you avoid circularity?
- Can you think just enough, then say or do?

Inspired by *The Smart Thinking Book*

ATTITUDE

ACTION

CREATIVITY

COMMUNICATION

EFFICIENCY

EMPATHY

STRATEGY

SUSTAINABILITY

4.10 LEARNING FROM MISTAKES

In the event of any miscommunication, I learn from my mistakes.

This is about acknowledging your imperfections and systematically addressing them. People and companies that shout too loudly and crow about their products and projects in a smug, superior way will inevitably attract the sceptics. It's much better to keep it real and involve your audience in the journey. Communicate with complete transparency. People will respect you and engage at a deeper level.

Every action has a reaction, and as you go along there is a high chance that you will make some mistakes, as everyone does. That's fine. The knack is to come clean and not try to hide them. You should:

- Acknowledge misjudgements as soon as possible.
- State exactly what happened.
- Explain why it was tricky.
- Outline what you have learned.
- Clarify what you are doing about it.

In many traditional forms of internal and external communication, the focus is on bigging up the company, using evocative and promotional language. By contrast, communicating with integrity requires a delicate balance between the heart and head – emotion and evidence. But the factual always needs to win out over the fanciful, so retain your humility and be prepared to admit that you are fallible.

Consider this
- Do you accept that humility is vital to empathy?
- Do you hide mistakes?
- Do you acknowledge misjudgements, learn from your mistakes and are prepared to explain what happened?

Inspired by *The Sustainable Business Book*

ATTITUDE

ACTION

CREATIVITY

COMMUNICATION

EFFICIENCY

EMPATHY

STRATEGY

SUSTAINABILITY

5. EFFICIENCY

> *"Methods are the most powerful truths of all."*
> Friedrich Nietzsche

True efficiency is hugely beneficial to both you and your bosses.

We start by explaining how not to be fooled by targets and plans that have little meaning, and why consistency in your work matters.

We move on to why it is essential to remove meaningless work from your action list and make clinical decisions.

It is important to take the initiative, choose the path of least resistance and take ownership of your tasks and projects.

We finish off by stressing the importance of doing all of this without the interference of others.

I set realistic targets. > HIT THE TARGET, MISS THE POINT	5.1
I deliver on my plans. > FICTIONAL PLANS	5.2
I put consistent effort into everything I do. > 20-MILE MARCH	5.3
I regularly review my ways of working. > AXE ADMINISTRIVIA	5.4
I am good at identifying what is truly possible. > THE DECISION WEDGE	5.5
I empower myself and colleagues to challenge and improve ways of working. > WHO'S GOING TO STOP ME?	5.6
I am good at prioritising tasks. > MINIMUM EFFORT, MAXIMUM IMPACT	5.7
I actively take responsibility for my projects. > PROBLEM OWNER, NOT PROBLEM MOANER	5.8
I give colleagues and teams regular and appropriate feedback about their work. > RADICAL CANDOUR	5.9
I remove distractions and interference to improve my concentration levels. > PERFORMANCE = ABILITY MINUS INTERFERENCE	5.10

ATTITUDE

ACTION

CREATIVITY

COMMUNICATION

EFFICIENCY

EMPATHY

STRATEGY

SUSTAINABILITY

5.1 HIT THE TARGET, MISS THE POINT

I set realistic targets.

> "All models are wrong, but some are useful."
> George Box, statistician

A target is just a target. It's something to aim at, but you might not hit it. A percentage is just a percentage. A percentage of what? One per cent of a lot might be a lot. Ninety-nine per cent of not very much might be ... not very much. So arbitrarily adding 10% to last year's target may well be pointless.

There is absolute performance and relative performance. Absolute performance is what *you* want to achieve. Relative performance compares yours with the competition. Do you really care what *they* do? Or would you rather concentrate on your own intentions and aspirations?

By all means, set targets, but do it on your own terms.

Consider this
- Are you fixated on targets?
- Can you ignore relative performance?
- Do you hit the target but miss the point?

Inspired by *The Smart Thinking Book*

5.2 FICTIONAL PLANS

I deliver on my plans.

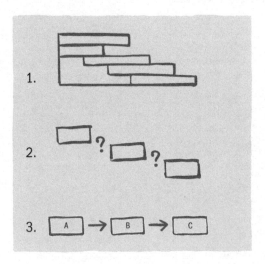

Businesses love to plan, and there is nothing particularly wrong with that. However, the problems begin when people start believing the plan. Some companies spend months planning, and eventually they will produce something that looks like 1.

Everyone gets very excited because the plan looks authoritative and is beautifully art directed. Everybody nods and walks out of the room under the impression that what is written on the plan is exactly what will happen. But it won't. So, a more realistic depiction of the plan might look something like 2.

If that's true, then a more iterative approach might be more honest, and ultimately more successful. In other words, don't allow the apparent authority of the beautifully crafted plan to convince you or the team that success is assured. Plan B is often better than Plan A, and accepting this possibility before everyone is emotionally and financially committed to plan A could save a lot of heartache. In which case, the plan may look like 3.

This is similar to iterative planning, but with a twist. In this version, the possibility of plans B and C are already built in to the strategic and planning process – not simply dreamt up at speed when plan A has not worked. This type of thinking reduces surprises. Part of this philosophy is an acknowledgement that most projects have a fuzzy front end – a period in which uncertainty should be expected and embraced, before clarity emerges.

The epitome of inefficiency is pursuing the wrong plan in full. Try some of these approaches to improve your efficiency.

Consider this
- Do you accept that plans don't normally come true?
- Do you allow them to make you believe they will happen?
- Could you go for flexible, iterative planning instead?

Inspired by *The Intelligent Work Book*

ATTITUDE

ACTION

CREATIVITY

COMMUNICATION

EFFICIENCY

EMPATHY

STRATEGY

SUSTAINABILITY

20-MILE MARCH

I put consistent effort into everything I do.

> *"Discipline, in essence, is consistency of action –*
> *consistency with values, consistency with long-term goals,*
> *consistency with performance standards, consistency of*
> *method, consistency over time."*
> Collins and Hansen, authors of *Great by Choice*

Polar explorer Roald Amundsen beat Captain Scott to the South
Pole by consistently marching 20 miles a day. He had worked out
in advance that 20 miles was the optimum amount for a team
with their equipment.

In bad weather the team did it anyway, and in good they stopped
at 20 to save energy for the next day. Scott's team either stayed
in their tents on bad days or overshot on good ones and wore
themselves out.

The moral is that companies, teams and individuals should aim for similar consistency. This is what the business authors Collins and Hansen call fanatic discipline. Don't ease off just because things are difficult or overdo it when things are easy. Apply consistent 20-mile marches, ask the same of your colleagues, and efficiency will improve.

Consider this
- Do you work out the optimum amount of effort needed?
- Do you often overshoot or undershoot on effort?
- Can you achieve consistency?

Inspired by *The Smart Thinking Book*

ATTITUDE

ACTION

CREATIVITY

COMMUNICATION

EFFICIENCY

EMPATHY

STRATEGY

SUSTAINABILITY

5.4 AXE ADMINISTRIVIA

I regularly review my ways of working.

> "If I stop to kick every barking dog, I'm not going to get where I'm going."
> Jackie Joyner-Kersee, Olympic athlete

Whoever heard someone say, *"What a great project that was – it took over 500 meetings to get it done"*?

Most people and companies have far too much to do. Or at least it appears that way. But much of what they are doing could be described as *administrivia*. The more tasks we are given, the more important it becomes to work out what is truly worth doing, and what is not.

Most status reports and activity sheets have far too much on them. This may make individuals and companies feel that they are being diligent. But in truth, it is more likely to be blurring their view of what really matters.

Concentrate on action, not activity. Cull as many projects and tasks as possible.

Often, one single action can utterly transform a project or task. Take the time to work out what that specific single action is, and just do that.

Consider this
- Do you often indulge in trivial comfort work?
- Can you distinguish between this and the important stuff?
- Can you concentrate on action not activity?

Inspired by *The Smart Thinking Book*

ATTITUDE

ACTION

CREATIVITY

COMMUNICATION

EFFICIENCY

EMPATHY

STRATEGY

SUSTAINABILITY

THE DECISION WEDGE

I am good at identifying what is truly possible.

The Decision Wedge is a useful way of looking at the merit of activities and projects. This technique analyses them based on whatever criteria you deem most important, but certainly on their practicality and ability to get done. That means making decisions on what to progress.

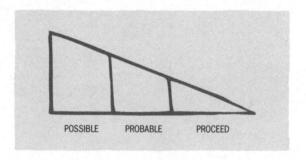

The possible section should include all the things that could possibly be enacted. This is not the same as the probable section, where the number is significantly reduced based on likelihood and available resource, which will naturally be finite. The proceed section does not necessarily mean that those things will be enacted, but it does mean that at this early stage, they are deemed sufficiently promising to proceed to the next development stage.

It is important that the number of activities or projects in each section is entirely realistic for you, a team, a department or the whole company, based on the resources it has at its disposal.

To use it, take all the possible items and screen them initially for practical possibility. Take a pause or involve some new people in the process. Now judge for probability – the likelihood of going ahead. Make sure the number in the proceed section is realistic. Then proceed.

Consider this
- Do you concentrate on everything that is possible?
- Can you reduce those options down to those that are probable?
- Can you then move something to the proceed level?

Inspired by *The Ideas Book*

5.6 WHO'S GOING TO STOP ME?

I empower myself and colleagues to challenge and improve ways of working.

You can be kind and considerate in your relationships, and that's fine. But you also need strength of purpose and sufficient conviction to stick to your guns when you encounter resistance to your approach. The Russian-American writer and philosopher Ayn Rand was tough on this:

> "The question isn't who is going to let me; it's who is going to stop me."
> Ayn Rand

However, this kind of approach to prevailing over the opinions of others comes with a health warning: tenaciously clinging on to a belief despite contrary evidence can be a mistake. Scientists and physicians are frequently guilty of this, putting up what Paul Feltovich calls 'knowledge shields' to allow them to stick to their original diagnoses even when subsequently proven wrong. Sense-check the elements in your approach(es) to ensure maximum efficiency. Then enact them to see immediate results.

Conviction is good, and overcoming resistance takes tenacity, so go for it.

Consider this
- Who's going to stop you?
- Do you have strength of purpose?
- Do you have the courage of your conviction?

Inspired by *The Smart Thinking Book*

5.7 MINIMUM EFFORT, MAXIMUM IMPACT

I am good at prioritising tasks.

A straightforward way to establish the effort needed to get tasks done is to use a *Minimum Effort, Maximum Impact* grid. This makes it easy to get your tasks in the right order of priority.

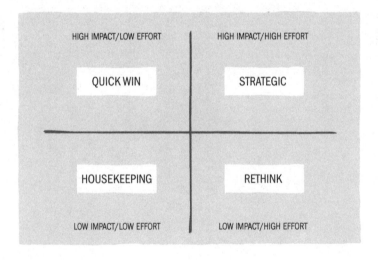

HIGH IMPACT/LOW EFFORT · HIGH IMPACT/HIGH EFFORT

QUICK WIN · STRATEGIC

HOUSEKEEPING · RETHINK

LOW IMPACT/LOW EFFORT · LOW IMPACT/HIGH EFFORT

First, identify early quick wins that require minimum effort but will deliver maximum impact. Do these first to make a solid start and establish momentum.

Second, make sure that all 'housekeeping' issues are attended to. They may be somewhat low impact, but they are also low effort, so get them done too.

Third, begin a strategic review of initiatives that will have a high impact but will involve a lot of effort. Consider these carefully and build them into long-term thinking.

And finally, if anything involves high effort but is likely, on reflection, to yield low impact, then why are you doing it? If this is the case, rethink.

Consider this
- Do you do the low effort stuff first?
- Can you then plan high effort stuff?
- Do you rethink high effort, low-impact tasks?

Inspired by *The Sustainable Business Book*

ATTITUDE

ACTION

CREATIVITY

COMMUNICATION

EFFICIENCY

EMPATHY

STRATEGY

SUSTAINABILITY

5.8 PROBLEM OWNER, NOT PROBLEM MOANER

I actively take responsibility for my projects.

OK, so it's a word play, but it works. Anyone can raise their eyeballs to the heavens and say, "Well, this is a big problem, isn't it?" These people are no help.

Someone needs to address the issue, taking responsibility and making suggestions about how to improve matters. Otherwise, we will all just sit around nodding sagely and confirming that there is, indeed, a problem. And if there is a problem, then that must be the worst kind of inertia to have.

Grab it by the scruff of the neck, work through some possible approaches and try something. Become a problem owner, not a problem moaner.

ATTITUDE

ACTION

CREATIVITY

COMMUNICATION

EFFICIENCY

EMPATHY

STRATEGY

SUSTAINABILITY

Tackling Problems: how we tackle problems is a good indicator of how we tackle life. Do you ignore the problem, hoping it will go away? Do you highlight the problem, but let it hang in the air, unresolved? Both have their issues. Ignoring the problem won't mean it magically disappears. By highlighting it, we may feel very clever for spotting it, but we are creating disruption without a solution. You need to understand the problem *and* work out how to solve it. You will be respected for your realistic and helpful approach.

Consider this
- Do you moan about things?
- Do you own the problem?
- Can you work out how to improve something?

Inspired by *The Excellence Book*

5.9 RADICAL CANDOUR

I give colleagues and teams regular and appropriate feedback about their work.

Giving and receiving feedback is a tricky business, but it is essential to improving efficiency. Most people are familiar with the shit sandwich – a nasty middle section preceded and followed by something apparently nice. According to Kim Scott in her book, *Radical Candor*, there is a better way to do it. Bosses can get what they want by saying what they mean – if they do it the right way.

Radical Candour means you have to care personally and challenge directly. Challenging directly without caring personally is just obnoxious aggression. Caring personally without challenging creates ruinous empathy. Neither caring nor challenging leads to manipulative insincerity. This matrix can be of benefit to both bosses and the person receiving the feedback – one for implementing, and the other to realise what the approach from the appraiser is.

Dawn Sillett, author of *The Feedback Book*, recommends the *EDGE* approach. **E**xplain: give a clear example of the behaviour that prompted the feedback. **D**escribe: the effect of that behaviour, the impact on others. **G**ive: them the microphone – invite them to speak. **E**nd: positively with encouragement and commitment.

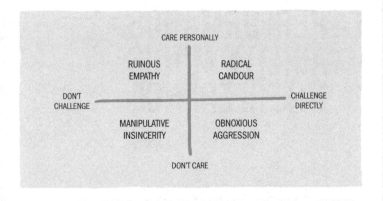

Often feedback sessions end in an impasse because the two parties do not agree. This is usually because the appraiser finds that the person being appraised has an apparently inaccurate opinion of their own capabilities. In the eyes of many subordinates, they feel that they are grafting away and getting little return for it. It feels like solid graft, with little return on recognition, financial reward or job satisfaction. Both parties would do well to discuss this blend and see if they can agree so that everyone is happy with the subsequent efficiency boost.

Consider this
- Do you care personally and challenge people directly?
- Do you avoid obnoxious aggression and ruinous empathy?
- Are you guilty of manipulative insincerity?

Inspired by *The Intelligent Work Book*

5.10 PERFORMANCE = ABILITY MINUS INTERFERENCE

I remove distractions and interference to improve my concentration levels.

According to Tim Gallwey, author of *The Inner Game of Tennis*, performance is ability minus interference. Ability means you can get the job done skillfully.

But we all know that even the best have bad days. Being worried or distracted debilitates your ability to concentrate and do things efficiently or well. So, on a personal level, if you want to do something well, remove all the distractions you can so you can get on and do your best.

Bosses and whole companies can learn from this, too. If an individual, or even an entire department, are to do something well, then they need to be allowed to get on with it.

Don't interfere: it reduces effective performance. Thanks to an array of modern devices, it is possible for people to contact us, and 'interfere' with our time, every second of the day. We have become *always on*. According to a University of California study, every time we are distracted, it takes 23 minutes and 15 seconds to get back to what we were working on. This means that if we are distracted four times an hour, we will not get anything done all day. It's easy to see how this would impede our performance. So, we need to limit this interference.

Ask yourself what interferes with you and what you can do to prevent it happening. Then put measures in place so that you can work efficiently.

Consider this
- Do you frequently get distracted?
- Do you distract others?
- Do you remove interference to improve performance?

Inspired by *The Excellence Book*

6. EMPATHY

> *"To pay attention, this is our endless and proper work."*
> Mary Oliver

Empathy takes numerous forms and is vital to the smooth and effective running of your life and business affairs.

We start by examining different character types and how they can work together, removing dysfunction and embracing diversity.

We move on to how important it is to allow for varied working styles, and the different types of thinking that follow from them.

It is important to view issues through the eyes of others, and to adjust your language to ensure a harmonious working atmosphere.

We finish off by highlighting the beneficial effects of taking thoughtful initiatives that benefit others and give you fulfilment in return.

I always foster a culture of trust and teamwork. > INTROVERTS, EXTRAVERTS AND AMBIVERTS	6.1
I recognise that my day-to-day behaviour helps shape the culture of the company I am in. > GETTING TACTILE	6.2
I can spot dysfunction in teams, and I always work to improve matters. > DEALING WITH DYSFUNCTION	6.3
I am strongly supportive of my company's diversity and inclusion efforts and initiatives. > EMBRACING DIVERSITY	6.4
I am comfortable working with people whose approaches are very different to mine. > MAKING WAY FOR THE MAVERICKS	6.5
I always create an environment that is conducive to generating a diverse range of opinions. > DIVERSE THINKING	6.6
I seek advice from outside my normal peer group to broaden my perspective. > EYES OF EXPERTS	6.7
I adjust my language to communicate with people in the most inclusive and empathetic way. > MIND YOUR LANGUAGE	6.8
I encourage people around me to pursue things that they feel strongly about. > INTRAPRENEURS	6.9
I actively support charitable activities. > SWEET CHARITY	6.10

ATTITUDE

ACTION

CREATIVITY

COMMUNICATION

EFFICIENCY

EMPATHY

STRATEGY

SUSTAINABILITY

6.1 INTROVERTS, EXTRAVERTS AND AMBIVERTS

I always foster a culture of trust and teamwork.

Teams need to be diverse, and that means different opinions and a range of working styles enacted empathetically. Psychologists have a seven-point scale to measure the range from introversion to extraversion. Some people claim they are one or the other, but the most important thing to note is that these are temporary mood states, not permanent ones. No one is an introvert 100% of the time. Or 100% extravert.

For example, it's a commonly held belief that extraverts make the best salespeople, but a study by Adam Grant at the University of Pennsylvania blew all that apart. His work was summarised succinctly by Daniel Pink in his book, *To Sell Is Human*.

The results on the next page show the sales performance of introverts on the left through to extraverts on the right. Perhaps not surprisingly, extreme introverts have difficulty selling effectively. But so do extreme extraverts, usually because they lack empathy and show destructive behaviour, such as an excess of zeal and assertiveness, and a desire to contact customers too frequently.

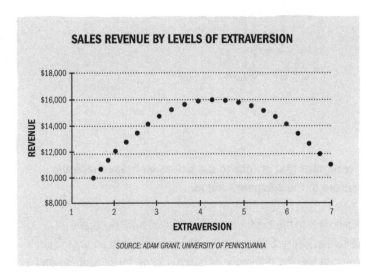

SALES REVENUE BY LEVELS OF EXTRAVERSION

REVENUE

$18,000
$16,000
$14,000
$12,000
$10,000
$8,000

1   2   3   4   5   6   7

EXTRAVERSION

SOURCE: ADAM GRANT, UNIVERSITY OF PENNSYLVANIA

Those that succeed best are *ambiverts*. This is not a trendy new buzzword. It has been around since the 1920s and is designed to describe those who can find the balance between being "geared to inspect" and "geared to respond." It's a powerful combination, and hopefully of great interest to introverts the world over.

Consider this
- Are you an introvert, an extravert, or a bit of both?
- Do you accept that extraversion and introversion are temporary states?
- Could you aspire to being an ambivert?

Inspired by *The Diagrams Book*

ATTITUDE

ACTION

CREATIVITY

COMMUNICATION

EFFICIENCY

EMPATHY

STRATEGY

SUSTAINABILITY

6.2 GETTING TACTILE

I recognise that my day-to-day behaviour helps shape the culture of the company I am in.

According to the book *Conscious Capitalism Field Guide* (Sisodia, Henry, Eckschmidt), when you walk into an organisation, you can feel the difference between a 'conscious' business and a traditional one, and this is down to culture.

The book promotes the TACTILE approach – an acronym representing seven qualities to consider:
- A high degree of *trust* permeates conscious businesses internally and externally with all stakeholders.
- *Authenticity* is essential to build trust.
- Feeling *cared for* and caring for others are core human needs.
- Conscious cultures are *transparent*, because there's little to hide.
- Strict adherence to truth-telling and fairness are at the heart of business *integrity*.
- A continual desire to *learn* helps businesses successfully evolve.
- Hire people with a strong fit to your company's culture and *empower* them to act intelligently and thoughtfully.

How TACTILE are you?

Trust	Are you trustworthy?
Authenticity	Are you truly authentic?
Caring	Do you make people feel cared for?
Transparency	Are you transparent with people?
Integrity	Do you act with integrity?
Learning	Do you encourage continual learning?
Empowerment	Do you make people around you feel empowered?

Consider this
- Does your day-to-day behaviour affect those around you?
- Do you have a positive impact on the culture of your business?
- How TACTILE are you?

Inspired by *The Ethical Business Book*

ATTITUDE

ACTION

CREATIVITY

COMMUNICATION

EFFICIENCY

EMPATHY

STRATEGY

SUSTAINABILITY

6.3 DEALING WITH DYSFUNCTION

I can spot dysfunction in teams, and I always work to improve matters.

Good businesses need functioning teams. There are five dysfunctions that can ruin the effectiveness and cohesion of any team, as outlined in the book *The Five Dysfunctions of a Team*, by Patrick Lencioni. Each dysfunction builds on the previous, making it even more difficult to isolate just one issue in a team. The foundation, however, needs to be trust – one of the most important elements of empathy in business practice. So, starting from the bottom (or foundation) of the pyramid and moving to the top, the important points are:

1. Absence of trust. Teams that are not open about mistakes and weaknesses make it impossible to build trust.
2. Fear of conflict. Teams that lack trust are incapable of engaging in unfiltered debate. Instead, they resort to veiled discussions and guarded comments.
3. Lack of commitment. Without having aired their opinions in open debate, team members rarely, if ever, buy in or commit to decisions.
4. Avoidance of accountability. Without committing to a clear plan of action, even the most focused people fail to call their peers to account.
5. Inattention to results. Failure to hold one another accountable creates an environment where team members put their individual needs above the team.

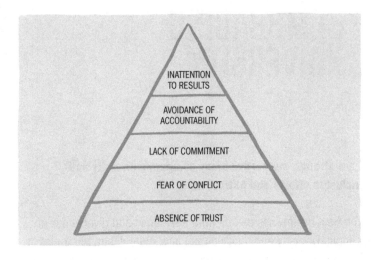

So, in conclusion:
- Trust comes from overcoming invulnerability and admitting to weaknesses.
- Constructive conflict needs to replace artificial harmony.
- Creating commitment means removing ambiguity.
- Accountability involves raising low standards.
- Inattention to results can be addressed by removing status and ego issues.

Consider this
- Do you struggle with absence of trust or fear of conflict?
- Does your team suffer from lack of commitment?
- Can you be vulnerable and have a robust discussion?

Inspired by *The Ethical Business Book*

6.4 EMBRACING DIVERSITY

I am strongly supportive of my company's diversity and inclusion efforts and initiatives.

The best businesses benefit from a dynamic and diverse mix of people. Diversity and inclusion are now, quite rightly, hot topics in business. But while many companies are talking about it, there is still a very long way to go. And all too often we see signs of 'divers-ish' practices – businesses being selectively inclusive, depending on what suits the organisation.

In her book *Diversify*, June Sarpong highlights how our general fear of the 'other' (whatever 'other' is for you) subconsciously influences our behaviour and reduces empathy. Whether we like it or not, 'other-ising' is something we all do, and 'other-isms' are something we all have. Here are some examples of different types of 'others':

The Other Man	Disenfranchised males in society.
The Other Woman	Gender inequality in society.
The Other Class	The economic gap between the elite and working class.
The Other Body	Treatment of those who don't fit the physical and mental standards of so-called 'able-bodied' people.

The Other Sex	How LGBTQ+ communities are treated.
The Other Age	Ageism from the perspective of young and old.
The Other View	Divisions caused by opposing political or religious views.

ATTITUDE
ACTION
CREATIVITY
COMMUNICATION
EFFICIENCY
EMPATHY
STRATEGY
SUSTAINABILITY

She proposes six degrees of integration:

1. Challenge your ism: beware of your conscious and unconscious bias.
2. Check your circle: don't just talk to the people you usually talk to.
3. Connect with the others: seek out people you wouldn't normally.
4. Change your mind: be prepared to accept another view.
5. Celebrate difference: find the best that alternative views can offer.
6. Champion the cause: there is more power in unity than division.

And try to avoid the cliché of male, pale and stale (or Yale) – an all-too-common scenario of male-orientated boardroom discussion and decision-making with no representation from minority groups.

Consider this
- Is your company 'divers-ish'?
- Do you consider others?
- Can you broaden your circle?

Inspired by *The Ethical Business Book*

6.5 MAKING WAY FOR THE MAVERICKS

I am comfortable working with people whose approaches are very different to mine.

According to Goffee and Jones in their book, *Clever*, you need brilliant people to run a great business or team and that means embracing the approaches of others that could be very different to your own. It is proven that a handful of star performers can create disproportionate amounts of value for their organisations, but it can be hard to establish empathy with them because although the 'clever ones' can be brilliant, they can also be difficult.

Their cleverness is central to their identity; their skills are not easily replicated; they know their worth; they ask difficult questions; they are organisationally savvy; they are not impressed by hierarchy; they expect instant success; they want to be connected to other clever people; and they won't thank you. They also take pleasure in breaking the rules. They can be oversensitive about their projects and are never happy about the review process.

So, traditional leadership approaches are often ineffective with them. Instead, bosses need to tell them what to do (not how to do it), earn their respect with expertise (not pull rank with a job title), and provide 'organised space' for their creativity. There is also an almost endless

DO ...	DON'T ...
Earn their respect with expertise, not a job title	Use hierarchy
Tell them what you want done	Tell them how to do it
Provide boundaries – organised space for creativity	Create bureaucracy
Give them time	Interfere
Give them recognition (amplify their achievements)	Give frequent feedback
Encourage failure and maximise learning	Train by rote (they are already highly skilled)
Talk straight	Intentionally deceive

Source: *Clever* (Goffee & Jones)

need to restate the company's purpose and verify that it aligns with what mavericks are being asked to do. Failure to do this will usually result in them pointing out the gap between strategy and execution.

Consider this
- Can you accommodate a wide variety of people?
- Are you broad minded?
- Do you allow for mavericks?

Inspired by *The Ethical Business Book*

ATTITUDE

ACTION

CREATIVITY

COMMUNICATION

EFFICIENCY

EMPATHY

STRATEGY

SUSTAINABILITY

6.6 DIVERSE THINKING

I always create an environment that is conducive to generating a diverse range of opinions.

Empathy needs a decent place to flourish, and yet many offices are sterile environments. Poor light, or no natural light. Airless basements. This is no place to foster an environment that encourages harmonious working and diverse thinking.

The famous explorer Thor Heyerdahl once answered a question like this.

> *"Borders? I have never seen one. But I have heard they exist in the minds of some people."*
> Thor Heyerdahl

This is a good metaphor for an open-minded approach to a wide range of views and opinions. Diverse thinking is stronger than just one view.

The French philosopher Simone Weil said, "Humility is attentive patience."

Humility goes a long way. And yet many managers are often strident, hectoring, macho and domineering. It's completely unnecessary. And it's not even an effective technique.

You might think that there are benefits to this approach, but there are none. So, companies should be in search of managers with modesty. People who don't have to show off regularly. Or brag incessantly. Or always take the credit. So, if you are forming a team, look for modesty. And if you are managing people, show some humility and spread the joy a bit to create an environment that promotes a diverse range of opinions.

Consider this
- Do you create an open-minded environment?
- Are you receptive to the views of others?
- Are you inquisitive and constructive?

Inspired by *The Smart Thinking Book*

ATTITUDE

ACTION

CREATIVITY

COMMUNICATION

EFFICIENCY

EMPATHY

STRATEGY

SUSTAINABILITY

6.7 **EYES OF EXPERTS**

I seek advice from outside my normal peer group to broaden my perspective.

This is a charming and fun technique that really helps to broaden your perspective, regardless of the topic. The idea is to view the world through the eyes of a known person who is very successful at something or known to have a particular stance. In this example, we have suggested a successful businessman, a sportsman and a universally known celebrity.

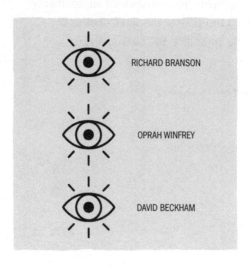

RICHARD BRANSON

OPRAH WINFREY

DAVID BECKHAM

It is not essential that they are technically expert, but it is important that they have a reputation for approaching their task in a distinctive way. The list of experts can be decided before a group session or generated spontaneously on the spot.

Then examine the issue or challenge using the style and viewpoint of each expert. This can either be done collectively, with all attendees imagining one expert at the same time, or separately by working through the eyes of several different ones. Capture the ideas and look at them straightaway or vet them later.

This is a fast and specific way of establishing empathy with a user group, customer base or partner organisation that you need to understand better.

Consider this
- Do you consider the perspectives of others?
- Do you think how somebody else would view this?
- Can you establish a broader view?

Inspired by *The Ideas Book*

ATTITUDE

ACTION

CREATIVITY

COMMUNICATION

EFFICIENCY

EMPATHY

STRATEGY

SUSTAINABILITY

6.8 MIND YOUR LANGUAGE

I adjust my language to communicate with people in the most inclusive and empathetic way.

Anyone who wishes to empathise with someone else needs to think carefully about the language they use. This applies whether you are a senior leader of a company or simply trying to explain your point of view. So, if your language is full of clichés, bull and the same old words we always see, it won't be impressive or endear you to whoever is listening.

Leaders who don't rehearse and think they can "riff off some slides," even when they haven't even seen them before, set a very bad example on this. In his book, *The Language of Leaders*, Kevin Murray says that inspiring language is vital to establishing a rapport with your audience, and he offers some suggestions:

- Create a clear and vivid view of the future and tell everybody.
- Engage and align people through conversations.
- Listen hard to inspire – be interested, respectful and patient.
- Stand up to stand out – you need a point of view.
- Use stories and anecdotes to motivate people.
- Don't send out signals that undermine your words.
- Prepare properly for public platforms – your reputation is at stake.
- Learn, rehearse, review, improve – always try to get better.

These are wise words for anyone wishing to empathise with others effectively. Whatever you say, keep it as short as possible.

TLDR stands for *Too Long, Didn't Read.*
TLDW stands for *Too Long, Didn't Watch.*

Consider this
- Do you listen carefully to what other people say?
- Do you adjust your language accordingly?
- Can you create a clear and vivid view of the future?

Inspired by *The Smart Strategy Book*

ATTITUDE

ACTION

CREATIVITY

COMMUNICATION

EFFICIENCY

EMPATHY

STRATEGY

SUSTAINABILITY

6.9 INTRAPRENEURS

I encourage people around me to pursue things that they feel strongly about.

Intrapreneurs are people on the payroll of medium to large businesses who opt of their own accord to take direct responsibility for initiatives that address social or ethical challenges, while also creating commercial value for the company. They are like entrepreneurs, but on the inside.

If you aspire to be such a person, build the following traits into your job.

A Learning Mindset
Learn as much as possible as quickly as possible and see everything you do as an opportunity to learn. Remove the stigma from mistakes and errors and view them as learning opportunities.

Trust in Yourself
Have a quiet confidence that you can take on whatever may come. Instead of fearing the unknown, develop trust that you can handle whatever challenge might be next.

ATTITUDE

ACTION

CREATIVITY

COMMUNICATION

EFFICIENCY

EMPATHY

STRATEGY

SUSTAINABILITY

Humility
Be open to other opinions, admit your mistakes, spend time in self-reflection and recognise that you can't do everything yourself. Accept blame and share praise. Trust others instead of micromanaging.

Resilience
Be tenacious and be creative.

Anyone can improve empathy at work, and everyone should try. Consider whether you want to step up and volunteer to get involved or lead cause-related activities such as the company's community day, charity event or diversity programme. This, in turn, can get you noticed, even if it's simply bumping into senior executives to get budgets signed off. It's a chance to shine, push entrepreneurial causes from the bottom up, and emote with others in a mutually beneficial way.

Consider this
- Do you encourage people to pursue what they feel strongly about?
- Do you encourage people to make things happen?
- Do you admire and reward initiative?

Inspired by *The Ethical Business Book*

6.10 SWEET CHARITY

I support charitable activities.

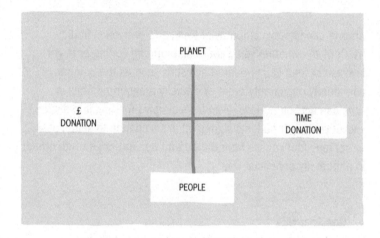

This simple grid can help you decide where to place your charity efforts – one of the ultimate manifestations of empathy. It can work on a personal level or determine the strategy for an entire company. The horizontal axis determines what degree of cash you are donating, as opposed to time. The vertical axis shows the balance of causes supported between the planet and people. Use it to have a discussion about what your approach should be.

Charity engagement has many benefits. It can cement your place in your local community, which in many cases will be positive for customer awareness, as well as generating good PR.

It is also very good for morale. Supporting events and charities that are close to your heart is great for employee engagement and establishing empathy. Many businesses have community engagement committees made up of employees that collectively decide on what the company should support and why. Employees can be encouraged to make suggestions or vote on options for even greater engagement. And, of course, if suitable initiatives do not currently exist, then you can consider starting one.

Giving back feels good, so consider your charity approach to improve your empathy.

Consider this
- Do you give something back?
- Do you support your community?
- If not money, can you help with time or product?

Inspired by *The Ethical Business Book*

ATTITUDE

ACTION

CREATIVITY

COMMUNICATION

EFFICIENCY

EMPATHY

STRATEGY

SUSTAINABILITY

7. STRATEGY

> "Rowing harder doesn't help if the boat is headed in the wrong direction."
> Kenichi Ohmae

Strategy is a hugely researched but widely misunderstood topic.

We start by defining it clearly and distinguishing it from tactics.

We move on to explain why it is important to think before you plan, stick to your principles, and map the market to find suitable opportunities.

Strategy is a complicated area, so we suggest a variety of ways to handle that complexity in relation to sales, customers and staff.

We finish off by outlining how to juggle the balance between the big picture and the detail.

I have a clear understanding of what a strategy is. > WHAT IS STRATEGY, ANYWAY?	7.1
I make a clear distinction between overall strategy and specific tactics. > STRATEGY OR TACTICS?	7.2
I know the difference between a strategy and a plan. > THINK BEFORE YOU PLAN	7.3
I know the difference between a strategy and a financial target. > PURSUE PRINCIPLES, NOT MONEY	7.4
I know how to create a commercial strategy. > GAP IN THE MARKET VS. MARKET IN THE GAP	7.5
I understand that selling isn't just for salespeople. > SALES: A DIRTY WORD?	7.6
I take strategy seriously. > RATIONAL DROWNING	7.7
I believe that customers need to be at the heart of any strategy. > CUSTOMERS ARE ALWAYS RIGHT	7.8
I am familiar with the principles of creating a people strategy. > PEOPLE POWER	7.9
I can switch between the big picture and specific actions without micromanaging the detail. > THE FINE-TOOTHED COMB	7.10

ATTITUDE

ACTION

CREATIVITY

COMMUNICATION

EFFICIENCY

EMPATHY

STRATEGY

SUSTAINABILITY

7.1 WHAT IS STRATEGY, ANYWAY?

I have a clear understanding of what a strategy is.

A strategy is a plan of action designed to achieve a long-term or overall aim. It is what you have decided to do. That's it. If anyone tries to tell you it's more complicated than that, then they are trying to mislead you.

There are many areas where a decent strategy will be of use. The most universal themes are:

Commercial: is it going to make money?
Brand: have we created a good one that people want to be associated with?
Customer: do we have a plan to reach them effectively?
Sales: can we generate enough and, if so, how?
People: how will our staff make all this thinking happen?
Innovation: can we come up with intelligent new ideas to help growth?
Communication: how will we explain all of this to colleagues, staff and customers?

All of this should be explainable on one sheet of paper, and sometimes even on a postcard. It is also worth remembering what a strategy is not:

It is not a long-winded discourse.
It is not a series of impenetrable charts.
It is not a drawing of the Parthenon populated by a long list of adjectives.
It is not a series of tactics cobbled together to suggest a unified thought.
It is not a verb, as in 'to strategise.'

Consider this
- Do you understand strategy?
- Can you work out what type of strategy you are working on?
- Can you keep it short and clear?

Inspired by *The Smart Strategy Book*

ATTITUDE
ACTION
CREATIVITY
COMMUNICATION
EFFICIENCY
EMPATHY
STRATEGY
SUSTAINABILITY

7.2 STRATEGY OR TACTICS?

I make a clear distinction between overall strategy and specific tactics.

One of the trickiest things businesses struggle with is the difference between strategy and tactics, and how to plan their shape. This Strategy vs. Tactics Year View helps clarify matters.

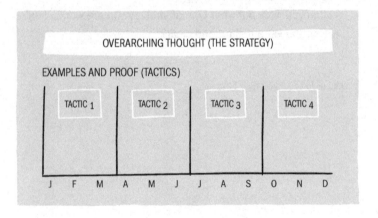

The strategy is the overarching thought, here shown as a top block or lintel. This is the consistent theme and direction that never varies, and against which all other activities can be judged and measured.

In some models, this is shown as a foundation. Both are acceptable, so long as their components remain constant.

With strategy, it's not what changes that matters – it's what stays the same. Because people like novelty, the temptation is to fiddle with everything, but it takes courage *not* to change something. The tactics are specific examples or proof of the strategy, and their deployment must have a clear beginning and end.

The year view helps clearly distinguish the two elements and enables you to map out precisely when the tactical initiatives should occur. Look at the year ahead. Decide on the overall strategy and place it as a constant overarching theme. Choose an appropriate number of tactics and place them in the right time segment. Look at the total picture and decide if it is suitably balanced. Use the year view to explain the plan to colleagues.

Consider this
- Do you agree that strategy is what you have decided to do?
- Do you accept that a series of tactics does not equal a strategy?
- Can you explain this clearly to others?

Inspired by *The Diagrams Book*

ATTITUDE

ACTION

CREATIVITY

COMMUNICATION

EFFICIENCY

EMPATHY

STRATEGY

SUSTAINABILITY

7.3 THINK BEFORE YOU PLAN

I know the difference between a strategy and a plan.

Strategy expert Max McKeown believes that thinking before you plan is vital. Strategists who don't take time to think are just planners. Strategy is all about shaping the future, and that requires a combination of thinking, planning and reacting to events that will undoubtedly emerge along the way. The crucial questions are:

What do we want to do?
What do we think is possible?
What do we need to do to achieve our goals?
When should we react to new opportunities and adapt plans?

Inspiration and insight can be drawn from looking forward, backward and outward, which often means blending smart prediction with past experience, and astute observation of what's happening outside the company and the category. Strategists need to know what stage their company, industry, products and services have reached. What crises have they survived? What will be next?

Survival is a priority, but growth is better. Consider questions such as this:

- How has the company grown in the past?
- What can fuel it in the future?
- Which markets and products could offer the greatest potential?

Just doing what you did last year isn't imaginative enough. This wide-ranging questioning must come before any semblance of a plan is constructed. Don't just dive in and write a plan. Many individuals and companies are fooled by plans. They think that because it is written down in an impressive way, then it must be a good strategy. This is sometimes called the 'spurious authority of type.' Somehow it all seems more convincing when it's typed up.

But that doesn't mean the strategy is any good. If you are drafting a strategy, use a pen and paper. The very last thing you should do is to make it look pretty. Are you staring at a strategy that looks impressive but lacks proper substance? If so, rip it up and think of something more original and effective.

Consider this
- Do you believe that a plan is not a strategy?
- Can you shape the future through your thinking?
- What do you think is truly possible?

Inspired by *The Smart Strategy Book*

ATTITUDE

ACTION

CREATIVITY

COMMUNICATION

EFFICIENCY

EMPATHY

STRATEGY

SUSTAINABILITY

7.4 PURSUE PRINCIPLES, NOT MONEY

I know the difference between a strategy and a financial target.

If your strategy boils down to a number, then the chances are it isn't a strategy. "To grow the business by 10%" is not a strategy. Nor is "To acquire x number of customers." That might be an objective or a desired outcome, but it's not the means by which you will get there. If the strategy is based on a number, it is probably ill-conceived. Numbers are not motivating in their own right. Start by getting the intent of the company or brand right and, if the strategy is a good one, the numbers will follow.

In his book, *Essentialism*, Greg McKeown explains the components of an essential intent. It needs to be both inspirational and concrete. For example, a vision or mission can be inspirational, but is rarely concrete. Quarterly objectives are concrete but never inspirational. Values are neither, and so are usually both general and bland. Inspiration isn't hard to identify, but it takes bravery.

The key to a concrete strategy is answering the question: *"How will we know when we're done?"* "A laptop for every child in Africa" is both concrete and inspirational. Good strategy pursues principles rather than just money.

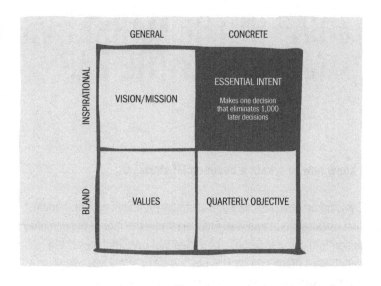

It is important to avoid any wishful thinking. For a strategy to really mean something, it will most likely embrace elements of sacrifice (what the company or brand won't do) and be genuine. You can only do that if it captures the imagination and is expressed well.

Consider this
- Do you acknowledge that a number is not a strategy?
- Do you believe that strategy is the hard art of standing apart?
- Can you avoid wishful strategic thinking?

Inspired by *The Smart Strategy Book*

7.5 GAP IN THE MARKET VS. MARKET IN THE GAP

I know how to create a commercial strategy.

Devising an effective commercial strategy requires careful thought and dispassionate analysis. Enthusiasm for the fate of the company is admirable, but hyperbolic language that overemphasises the capabilities of the company is not. Too many strategists exaggerate the possibilities available, but they would be better off being realistic.

The first thing to do is map the market. Start by selecting the two most important factors in the market, then plot two perpendicular axes (one for each factor) from high to low and place your company or brand and any competitors on the grid. Use the results to identify gaps in the market or significant overlaps.

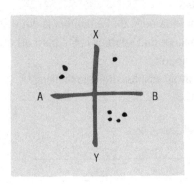

Being out on your own could either be good (more distinctive) or bad (in the wrong territory). Being with too many other brands is usually too cluttered, just like schoolchildren all chasing a ball. But beware fool's gold. Fool's gold looks like gold, but it isn't. It is usually some other yellow mineral, such as pyrite or chalcopyrite. White space is blank, and when it's on a strategist's market map, it makes them think that there's a gap to be exploited. But they might be wrong.

There is, apparently, a gap in the market, but is there a market in the gap? Brand strategists need to ponder this question very carefully before making recommendations too hastily. The apparent gap could simply be a failure masquerading as a viable opportunity.

Many strategists knock up a market map and triumphantly declare that they have spotted a gap in the market. But they might be too hasty – and wrong. After generating this initial view of the brand position, good strategists must ask two vital questions: (1) Why is this space unoccupied? and (2) What do others know that we don't?

The so-called gap may be there for a very good reason, so look carefully at the flaws of that position in the market and at any previous attempts by competitors to occupy that area. Chances are someone has made the same mistake already, so you can avoid it.

Consider this
- Can you map the market?
- Is there a market in the gap?
- Can you avoid the pitfalls of fool's gold white space?

Inspired by *The Smart Strategy Book*

ATTITUDE

ACTION

CREATIVITY

COMMUNICATION

EFFICIENCY

EMPATHY

STRATEGY

SUSTAINABILITY

7.6 SALES: A DIRTY WORD?

I understand that selling isn't just for salespeople.

These four mantras shed some light on different types of sales strategy. Selling isn't just for salespeople – everyone in the company should be contributing and should know how to explain what the company does in a persuasive way. Successful selling is challenging – challenging what the requester has asked for is one of the most effective ways to involve them and persuade them to buy from you. New business can be old business – do not neglect current and old customers who may offer easier routes to success with lower levels of resistance. And beware the strategy/execution gap – the strategy doesn't count if you haven't enacted it.

In one or two exceptional cases, customer demand is so high that a company barely has to make an effort to sell their stuff. This is extremely rare, so for everyone else, a successful selling approach is needed. And that means an effective sales strategy.

But in some countries, notably Great Britain, 'sales' is a dirty word. Even in the US, the home of overt selling, people spontaneously come up with words such as pushy, sleazy, annoying and manipulative to describe sales or selling (*To Sell Is Human*, Daniel Pink). But in truth, we are all selling most of the time.

Want me to agree with you? Sell me your thought. Want me to meet you at a certain place? Sell me your proposed venue. You get the idea.

Companies can no longer sell to people in a crass way. Customers need to want to buy, so making a sale may be a complicated conversation with many angles.

Investigate all angles before proceeding.

- Selling isn't just for salespeople.
- Successful selling is challenging.
- New business can be old business.
- Beware the strategy/execution gap.

Consider this
- Do you think sales is a dirty word?
- Can you sell in one form or another?
- Can you make customers want to buy?

Inspired by *The Smart Strategy Book*

ATTITUDE

ACTION

CREATIVITY

COMMUNICATION

EFFICIENCY

EMPATHY

STRATEGY

SUSTAINABILITY

7.7 RATIONAL DROWNING

I take strategy seriously.

Some sales strategies rely on a relentlessly cheerful approach. But in many contexts, this is counterproductive. In fact, it can pay to suggest that the issue is much harder than the potential customer believes. Sometimes this involves taking the mood down for a short while to emphasise the severity of the problem. This is followed by bringing the customer back up with your proposed solution. This is called 'rational drowning.' According to authors Dixon and Adamson in their book, *The Challenger Sale*, effective commercial teaching usually involves six main stages.

1. ***Warmer:*** build credibility through empathy.
2. ***Reframing:*** shock the customer with the unknown.
3. ***Rational drowning:*** intensify the problem and then break it down.
4. ***Emotional impact:*** make the problem human.
5. ***Value proposition:*** introduce a new way, building confidence back up.
6. ***Solution and implementation map:*** describe in detail how to fix the problem with your product.

'Hypothesis-based selling' involves leading with a hypothesis of the customer's needs, informed by experience and research.

Bear in mind that having widespread support across an organisation is now vital to likely sales success – going straight to the decision maker is unlikely to work.

KPMG has an interesting SAFE-BOLD framework that allows you to score from 1–10 the scale, risk, innovativeness and difficulty of any sales issue.

SAFE = Small, Achievable, Following, Easy
BOLD = Big, Outperforming, Leading edge, Difficult.

Interestingly, the sales experience contributes more to customer loyalty (53%) than the brand (19%), product and service delivery (19%) and value-to-price ratio (9%) put together, so it is really worth getting it right.

Don't use rational drowning if the sales context is relatively simple. There's no need to frighten the horses if everything is pretty straightforward. Bear in mind that many companies think that things are more complicated than they truly need to be. Many potential customers have a high level of understanding already, so it pays to understand how sophisticated your audience is and pitch your sales strategy accordingly.

Consider this
- Do you consider the true complexity of the task?
- Can you explain how complicated it is?
- Can you offer an intelligent solution?

Inspired by *The Smart Strategy Book*

ATTITUDE

ACTION

CREATIVITY

COMMUNICATION

EFFICIENCY

EMPATHY

STRATEGY

SUSTAINABILITY

7.8 CUSTOMERS ARE ALWAYS RIGHT

I believe that customers need to be at the heart of any strategy.

You can be the best-organised company in the world, have the most advanced products and amazing branding, but without customers, a company amounts to nothing. So it pays to have an excellent customer strategy. However, many strategies are found wanting when it comes to their candid depiction of customers and exactly where they are going to come from.

Many are described as consumers – as though they eat the product? Many are categorised as a target audience – as though you can fire things at them? Some are clustered into imaginary and often condescending typologies – Deborah from Walthamstow, anyone?

Much of this work is too fanciful and conveniently ignores the stark reality that a customer is just someone who buys your stuff. And their behaviour can be very hard to predict. A robust customer strategy will usually involve reliable and accurate research, working out the difference between loyal customers and those who may be prepared to go elsewhere, and understanding the sometimes-strange decisions that customers make.

Beware misleading research. The data you see is often hiding deeper issues. Avoid the thinking/doing gap. If it can't be done, then it merely remains theoretical. Beware disloyal loyalists. People can be 'loyal' to more than one company or brand. And you don't always have to think big. Small changes can have a big effect, so concentrate hard on formulating an intelligent customer strategy.

- Beware misleading research.
- Avoid the thinking/doing gap.
- Beware disloyal loyalists.
- Small changes can have a big effect.

Consider this
- Can you avoid being misled by research?
- Can you avoid unhelpful typologies?
- Exactly who is going to buy your stuff?

Inspired by *The Smart Strategy Book*

ATTITUDE

ACTION

CREATIVITY

COMMUNICATION

EFFICIENCY

EMPATHY

STRATEGY

SUSTAINABILITY

7.9 PEOPLE POWER

I am familiar with the principles of creating a people strategy.

We talk of companies, corporations, boards and brands. But they are all made up of people, so a sensitive people strategy is extremely important. It has become fashionable to describe workforces variously as human resources or human capital. These descriptors have a strangely distancing effect. We are, after all, still talking about people. And people are very varied. They can be viewed by job title, by department or as individuals.

Bosses can either be brilliant or ruin everything. So can members of staff. It's the interplay between the leaders and the rest that holds the key to success or failure. People strategy needs to be looked at from all angles: from the overall company approach, to how the leaders should behave, to how individuals can perform to the best of their ability. Managing people requires clear thinking and courageous action to ensure organisational health and get everyone working together effectively, based on trust and effective teamwork.

Consider these elements. Manage the people, not the numbers. Good results flow from happier people. Clear thinking and courageous action make a huge difference. Vagueness and delay are hugely demoralising. Ensure organisational health. Measure staff morale regularly and top it up as often as possible. And get people in flow. Leave them to do high-quality, uninterrupted work.

Drawing all this together generates a people strategy – one of the most important documents in any company.

- Manage the people, not the numbers.
- Nurture clear thinking and courageous action.
- Ensure organisational health.
- Get people in flow.

Consider this
- Do you agree that companies are just made up of people?
- Can you look carefully at everything from all angles?
- Do you put people first?

Inspired by *The Smart Strategy Book*

ATTITUDE

ACTION

CREATIVITY

COMMUNICATION

EFFICIENCY

EMPATHY

STRATEGY

SUSTAINABILITY

7.10 THE FINE-TOOTHED COMB

I can switch between the big picture and specific actions without micromanaging the detail.

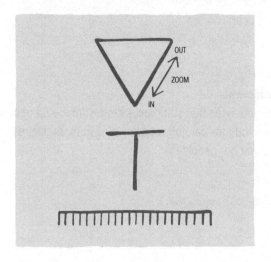

Modern business comes with a built-in dilemma: how to cope with the big picture and the detail at the same time. This is an issue that vexes business leaders. On the one hand, they are concerned with the overall strategic direction of a company and, on the other, they are perpetually dragged into specific operational detail.

The knack is to be able to zoom in and zoom out fast, all day, every day. Zooming out reveals the big picture, and zooming in shows the detail. The first is all about widening options and attaining distance. The second is all about understanding the true operational or technical detail. This idea was originally suggested by Collins and Hansen in their book, *Great by Choice*.

There are dangers on both sides of this dilemma. Those who consistently talk about strategy (the so-called big picture) are often accused of generalising too much and failing to understand the detail. Those who zoom in too much are often seen as micromanaging or being too down in the weeds. A flexible balance is needed. This is why T-shaped executives are so highly valued. The crossbar of the T demonstrates their broad understanding of a business, and the vertical shows their deep specific knowledge.

And in multifaceted businesses, a successful manager may have to become adept on many fronts – a series of Ts in a row, with a profile more like a fine-toothed comb, in which they constantly review both big strategic issues and small executional details.

Consider this
- Can you constantly review both big and small issues?
- Can you zoom in and out between the two frequently?
- Do you become obsessed with the detail?

Inspired by *The Intelligent Work Book*

ATTITUDE

ACTION

CREATIVITY

COMMUNICATION

EFFICIENCY

EMPATHY

STRATEGY

SUSTAINABILITY

8. SUSTAINABILITY

> "Unless someone like you cares a whole awful lot,
> nothing is going to get better. It's not."
> Dr. Seuss

Sustainability is an essential subject that should be at the heart of every business and individual.

We start by mapping out why it is such an important topic and how to understand your own carbon footprint.

We move on to explaining the global context and what it all means for business.

We offer our take on it by introducing a concept that we call eco-nomics and map out all the important elements of it.

We finish off by demonstrating how everyone can stop, think, and challenge their behaviour for the good, and avoid inappropriate greenwashing of these vital issues.

I fully understand the implications of climate change. > A HOT TOPIC	8.1
I understand my own carbon footprint. > TREADING LIGHTLY	8.2
I am familiar with the global ambitions relating to sustainability. > SUSTAINABLE DEVELOPMENT GOALS	8.3
I understand why sustainability is important to business performance. > THE NEW BUSINESS REALITY	8.4
I believe business exists for more than just the pursuit of profit. > INTRODUCING ECO-NOMICS	8.5
I try not to put short-term gain ahead of long-term sustainable development. > PEOPLE, PLANET, PROFIT	8.6
Having a strong moral purpose is important to me. > THE POINT OF PURPOSE	8.7
I am familiar with the principles of the circular economy. > GOING AROUND IN CIRCLES	8.8
I believe that sustainability is everyone's responsibility. > STOP, THINK, CHALLENGE	8.9
I am conscious of greenwashing, both in terms of my own company's products and when buying products from other people. > GREENWASH ALERT	8.10

ATTITUDE

ACTION

CREATIVITY

COMMUNICATION

EFFICIENCY

EMPATHY

STRATEGY

SUSTAINABILITY

A HOT TOPIC

I fully understand the implications of climate change.

Although sustainability is about a lot more than just the green stuff, climate change is central to our environmental stewardship, which is why it is now such a hot topic.

Climate change refers to long-term shifts in temperatures and weather patterns. Some shifts may be natural, through variations in the solar cycle, but the impact of human activities is now the main driver of climate change.

This is due to an increased concentration of greenhouse gases (GHGs) in the Earth's atmosphere, such as carbon dioxide (CO_2), methane (CH_4), and nitrous oxide (N_2O).

These gases trap heat from the sun, creating what is known as the greenhouse effect. Human activities, particularly the burning of fossil fuels (coal, oil and natural gas) for energy production, transportation and industrial processes, are the primary sources of these emissions.

As a result of climate change, the Earth's average temperature has been rising, with a range of negative impacts.

These impacts will be unevenly felt around the world, with some countries facing far greater risks than others. However, given our globalised food systems and the increased political instability from conflict over resources, all countries, communities and companies will feel the impacts and costs of climate change.

Increase in heat-related events such as heat waves, hurricanes, storms, wildfires, and drought.

Increasingly unpredictable rainfall with floods in some areas and droughts in others.

Melting of glaciers and ice caps, leading to rising sea levels, which threatens coastal areas, increases risk of flooding and endangered ecosystems and communities.

Disruption to ecosystems due to changes in climate conditions affecting habitats, migration patterns and increased risk of species extinction.

Agricultural disruption resulting in failed crops, altering growing seasons, and increased risk of pests and disease.

Consider this
- What does climate change mean to you?
- Have you researched it to a sensible level?
- Can you view it in a business context?

Inspired by *The Sustainable Business Book*

ATTITUDE

ACTION

CREATIVITY

COMMUNICATION

EFFICIENCY

EMPATHY

STRATEGY

SUSTAINABILITY

TREADING LIGHTLY

I understand my own carbon footprint.

CO_2 is shorthand for carbon dioxide. It is one of the seven major greenhouse gases (GHGs) that contribute to climate change. CO_2e is shorthand for carbon dioxide equivalent. This covers all greenhouse gas emissions that contribute to climate change, including carbon dioxide (CO_2), methane (CH_4), nitrous oxide (N_2O), and refrigerant gases like hydrofluorocarbons (HFCs). Using CO_2e makes it easy to compare the impact of a range of activities.

To combat climate change, we need to reduce carbon emissions. And to reduce carbon emissions, we need to understand them.

To give you a flavour, here are some estimated examples from *How Bad Are Bananas?* by Mike Berners-Lee.

Berners-Lee suggests that a five-ton lifestyle is the working target for the amount of CO_2e an average UK person should contribute per year.

As it currently stands, the 'average' global citizen has a footprint of seven tons, but it varies hugely – for example, the average American footprint is 21 tons, in the UK it is 13 tons and in Malawi just 0.2 tons.

ATTITUDE

ACTION

CREATIVITY

COMMUNICATION

EFFICIENCY

EMPATHY

STRATEGY

SUSTAINABILITY

Travelling one mile...	CO_2e
By pedal bike (powered by bananas)	40 g
By bus (London Routemaster – half-full diesel hybrid)	46 g
By train (intercity – standard class)	80 g
By petrol car (average UK car)	530 g
General	CO_2e
A cup of black tea	22 g
A large cows' milk latte	552 g
A toilet roll (virgin paper)	730 g
A paperback book	1 kg
Taking a generous bath (heated by an efficient gas boiler)	1 kg
A pint of cows' milk	1.1 kg
A 10-inch Margherita pizza	1.4 kg
A beef cheeseburger	3.2 kg
A week's food shopping (vegan, no airfreight, no waste)	17 kg
An average week's food shopping (including meat, airfreight)	88 kg
Flying	CO_2e
Return flight – London to Hong Kong (economy)	3.5 tons
Return flight – London to Hong Kong (business)	10 tons

Source: *How Bad Are Bananas?*, Mike Berners-Lee

Overleaf are some effective ways to tread more lightly by lowering your carbon footprint at home. Many of these actions also benefit nature and/or reduce waste. They may also save you money.

To calculate your personal carbon footprint, visit www.footprint.wwf.org.uk.

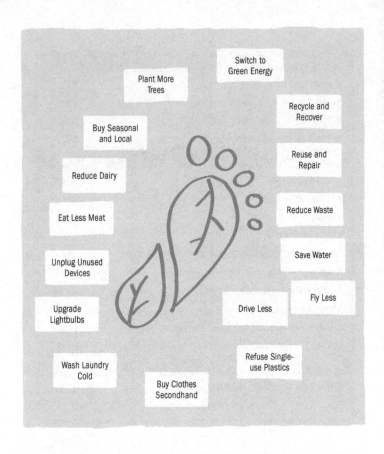

Switch to Green Energy

Plant More Trees

Recycle and Recover

Buy Seasonal and Local

Reuse and Repair

Reduce Dairy

Reduce Waste

Eat Less Meat

Save Water

Unplug Unused Devices

Fly Less

Upgrade Lightbulbs

Drive Less

Wash Laundry Cold

Refuse Single-use Plastics

Buy Clothes Secondhand

Consider this
- Have you worked out your personal carbon footprint?
- How can you tread more lightly?
- Can you influence your business in a similar way?

Inspired by *The Sustainable Business Book*

SUSTAINABLE DEVELOPMENT GOALS

I am familiar with the global ambitions relating to sustainability.

When looking at global sustainability ambitions, the best place to start is the 2030 Agenda for Sustainable Development, adopted by United Nations Member States in 2015. At its heart are the 17 Sustainable Development Goals (SDGs).

These 17 SDGs recognise that "ending poverty and other deprivations must go hand-in-hand with strategies that improve health and education, reduce inequality and spur economic growth – all while tackling climate change and working to preserve our oceans and forests."

This really helps us understand the interconnection between people and the planet. We need to balance our efforts to ensure a healthy planet that is safe and equitable for all of us to live on. By reviewing the SDGs, you can draw inspiration about areas where you can make a real difference.

For more details on the Sustainable Development Goals, visit www.un.org/sustainabledevelopment.

If they feel a little overwhelming, check out the World Business Council for Sustainable Development's Good Life Goals. These outline personal actions that everyone around the world can take to help support the SDGs,

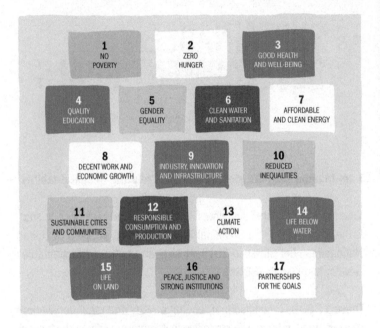

including a guide to how businesses can make the goals relevant to employees and customers.

For more details on the Good Life Goals,
visit www.sdghub.com/goodlifegoals.

Consider this
- Have you worked through the SDGs to understand global ambitions?
- Have you looked at the Good Life Goals?
- How can you use these as inspiration in your own life?

THE NEW BUSINESS REALITY

ATTITUDE

ACTION

CREATIVITY

COMMUNICATION

EFFICIENCY

EMPATHY

STRATEGY

SUSTAINABILITY

I understand why sustainability is important to business performance.

> *"Every pound spent is a vote for how we want to live."*
> Mary Portas

Against the backdrop of an urgent need for more sustainable development, every area of society, government and legislation is now under scrutiny. And, increasingly, people are pressing for change. Intelligent companies realise that the very people agitating for change hold the key to a prosperous future.

THE NEW CONSCIOUS CONSUMER

Conscious consumers want to purchase goods and services they perceive to be less harmful to the planet and better for society in general. This is on the increase as consumers become more and more aware of the harsh realities associated with many brands and products, such as excessive use of fossil fuels, deforestation, tax avoidance, unacceptable working conditions and modern slavery.

BUSINESS TO BUSINESS

Most companies are part of a supply chain, and many contracts now rest on proven sustainability credentials. Failure to provide them often leads to exclusion from the ability to tender for contracts when responding to a Request for Proposal. Businesses looking to de-risk their own supply chain put pressure on their suppliers to improve their sustainability status.

EMPLOYEES

More and more employees place deep importance on sustainability – particularly the younger generations of Millennials and Gen Z. The sustainability agenda (such as workers' rights, well-being and diversity) affects the recruitment and loyalty of staff, the actions they take and the career decisions they make. Unethical and uncaring companies either lose or fail to attract the best and brightest talent.

INVESTORS

It is no longer acceptable for investors to commit their money to companies with dubious practices. Even ignoring their financial objectives, many are under legislative pressure that forces them to improve standards. Any business currently building to sell will be aware of the pressure to build a robust ESG strategy into value creation and exit planning. Similarly, those seeking investment should expect deep scrutiny in this area.

In the past, businesses have judged their competitive advantages based on three components: price, quality and convenience. Modern businesses now realise that you can compete on each of those areas, but if your product or service lacks strong evidence of sustainability, you will lose out to others in your market when it comes to customers, talent and investment.

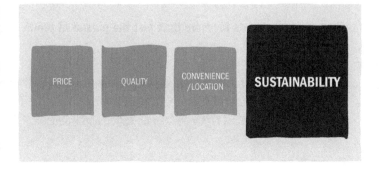

Consider this
- Have you considered how your customers' needs are changing?
- Do you believe that sustainability is crucial to your business in the future?
- How can you use this understanding?

Inspired by *The Sustainable Business Book*

ATTITUDE

ACTION

CREATIVITY

COMMUNICATION

EFFICIENCY

EMPATHY

STRATEGY

SUSTAINABILITY

8.5 INTRODUCING ECO-NOMICS

I believe business exists for more than just the pursuit of profit.

> *"The transition to net zero is creating the greatest commercial opportunity of our age."*
> Mark Carney, UN Special Envoy on Climate Action and Finance

Profit is not in itself a bad thing – businesses need to be commercially viable. It's how you make the profit and what you do with it that matters. But the relentless pursuit of profit over caring for people and the planet is not good, and it's bad for business too (see 8.4).

The old way is a scenario in which the owner or investor is in the predominant role, exploiting resources for money. For this idea, many blame the economist Milton Friedman, who in the 1970s asserted that the purpose of a company is to make money for shareholders.

If your business is solely focused on profit, then you are in essence saying that you care more about money than you do about your customers or your employees (on which the business completely relies). This type of old-fashioned, money-based thinking has been challenged, along with many other aspects of old business thinking.

The authors have written regularly on this topic and originally coined the term Ethicalnomics to encapsulate the new thinking required. After a discussion in which a good friend, Jon Howard, suggested the brilliant term Enoughonomics, we have arrived at Eco-nomics with a simple hyphen to make the distinction, as a descriptor for the new model.

The Eco-nomics model challenges old business thinking, starting with the perceived conflict between making money and doing good. The model expresses the changes needed in businesses to head them in the right direction.

Economics → Ethicalnomics → Enoughonomics → Eco-nomics

The model encourages a move away from the traditional drive for uncontrolled growth to good growth, green growth or even degrowth.

It encourages taking the long view, rather than short-termism, and ditching the traditional single bottom line in favour of the triple bottom line of people, planet and profit (see 8.6).

It promotes circular thinking rather than the take-make-waste approach (see 8.8), ditching fossil fuels in favour of renewable energy sources, and creating sustainable supply chains over exploitative, price-only based practices.

In a world of so much overconsumption, the model recommends being more mindful about purchasing and usage, along with a new approach to marketing that is less focused on fuelling consumer demand and more on integrity (with no greenwashing – see 8.10).

ATTITUDE

ACTION

CREATIVITY

COMMUNICATION

EFFICIENCY

EMPATHY

STRATEGY

SUSTAINABILITY

Above all, it suggests a new approach to leadership, moving from a selfish and ego-centric style to one that is nurturing and eco-centric.

FROM Economics	TO Eco-nomics
Infinite growth	**Good growth**
Short-term thinking	**Long-term perspective**
Financial-only reporting	**Triple bottom line**
Linear	**Circular**
Fossil fuels	**Renewable energy**
Fastest, cheapest supplies	**Sustainable supply chains**
Overconsumption	**Mindful consumption**
Sales-at-any-cost marketing	**Responsible marketing**
Ego-leadership	**Eco-leadership**

Consider this
- Do you put profit above everything else?
- Do you challenge all aspects of your business?
- Can you start practicing Eco-nomics?

Inspired by *The Sustainable Business Book*

8.6 PEOPLE, PLANET, PROFIT

ATTITUDE

ACTION

CREATIVITY

COMMUNICATION

EFFICIENCY

EMPATHY

STRATEGY

SUSTAINABILITY

I try not to put short-term gain ahead of long-term sustainable development.

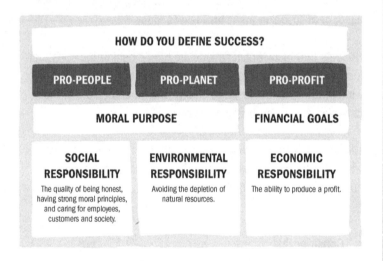

HOW DO YOU DEFINE SUCCESS?

PRO-PEOPLE	PRO-PLANET	PRO-PROFIT
MORAL PURPOSE		FINANCIAL GOALS
SOCIAL RESPONSIBILITY The quality of being honest, having strong moral principles, and caring for employees, customers and society.	**ENVIRONMENTAL RESPONSIBILITY** Avoiding the depletion of natural resources.	**ECONOMIC RESPONSIBILITY** The ability to produce a profit.

Many businesses still see sustainability as a necessary evil – something they must now do, whether they like it or not. Others, however, are seeing this as an opportunity to change the way business views success, redressing the bias toward the relentless pursuit of profit with little regard for the health of people and the planet (see 8.5).

Rather than focusing on just the traditional bottom line, responsible businesses are adopting the Triple Bottom Line – People, Planet and Profit. This was a term first coined by sustainability pioneer John Elkington. It describes a business model that forces companies to focus not just on money, but also on high business integrity and environmental sensitivity, resulting in both successful business strategy and moral business practice.

It should be noted that in his 2020 book, Green Swans, Elkington talks of retracting the concept of the Triple Bottom Line – not because it is bad, but because he is dismayed by how it is being used, or misused, in many businesses today.

He feels that many organisations are hiding behind the construct, just paying lip service to it and using it as a tick box exercise without any genuine desire to change the fundamentals of their commercially driven business models.

Like so much surrounding sustainability, to create real change with integrity, it is important to embark on this with genuine commitment, not just for PR purposes.

Consider this
- Have you adopted a triple bottom line approach?
- How can you report on your nonfinancial achievements?
- Are you doing this for the right reason and with integrity?

Inspired by The Sustainable Business Book

ATTITUDE

ACTION

CREATIVITY

COMMUNICATION

EFFICIENCY

EMPATHY

STRATEGY

SUSTAINABILITY

8.7 THE POINT OF PURPOSE

Having a strong moral purpose is important to me.

There is much talk about purpose in business these days, but what does it mean?

In short, your moral purpose should be greater than the products you make or the services you provide. This works on both a personal and an organisational level.

At the heart of establishing a wider moral purpose for your business is the recognition that doing good and making money are not incompatible.

Knowing what intrinsically motivates your people, what you are built to do better than anyone else, and where you can deploy that passion and talent to serve a need or solve a problem in the world is extremely powerful.

This matrix is from the book *Conscious Capitalism Field Guide* (Sisodia, Henry, Eckschmidt) and provides an excellent framework for establishing where your moral purpose is or should be.

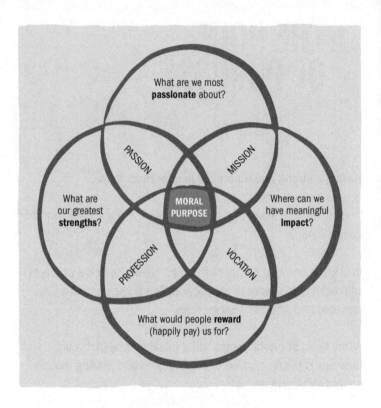

1. What is your business's greatest strength? What do you have the potential to be the best at in the world?
2. What are we most passionate about? What do you love the most about what you do?
3. Where can you have the most meaningful impact? Which big problems or needs in the world are you capable of solving?
4. What would people reward you for? What products and services would your customers happily pay for (maybe even a little more if you could deliver them in a more ethical fashion)?

By answering these questions diligently and honestly, a company can get considerably closer to defining its moral purpose and working out what specific actions are needed to enact it.

Consider this
- What are you most passionate about?
- Where can you have the most impact?
- Are you doing all this for the right reason?

Inspired by *The Ethical Business Book*

ATTITUDE

ACTION

CREATIVITY

COMMUNICATION

EFFICIENCY

EMPATHY

STRATEGY

SUSTAINABILITY

8.8 GOING AROUND IN CIRCLES

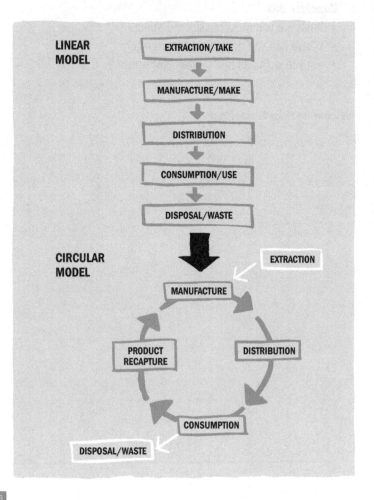

LINEAR MODEL

EXTRACTION/TAKE

MANUFACTURE/MAKE

DISTRIBUTION

CONSUMPTION/USE

DISPOSAL/WASTE

CIRCULAR MODEL

EXTRACTION

MANUFACTURE

DISTRIBUTION

PRODUCT RECAPTURE

CONSUMPTION

DISPOSAL/WASTE

I am familiar with the principles of the circular economy.

At the heart of a lot of sustainability thinking is the recognition that we need to embrace a more circular way of thinking. The circular economy model is inspired by natural living systems and promotes the fact that there is no such thing as waste in nature. Unlike the traditional linear approach of take-make-use-waste, a circular economy is a sustainable closed-loop model.

It creates value through product recapture and then recycling, restoring and reusing product elements in remanufacturing – thereby radically limiting the extraction of raw materials at the beginning, and the production of waste at the end, of a product's life.

In essence, it involves keeping products and materials in use for as long as possible. This is driving new trends in repurposing items, easy home repair and the increase in second-hand (or pre-loved) purchasing.

The circular economy concept also challenges the necessity of owning products in the way that we are traditionally used to. It is access to what the product provides that is important, rather than the product itself. Understanding this shift in mindset lays the groundwork for shifting our economy from linear to circular and can be seen in many examples now, from car sharing clubs to fashion rental.

ATTITUDE

ACTION

CREATIVITY

COMMUNICATION

EFFICIENCY

EMPATHY

STRATEGY

SUSTAINABILITY

Intelligent modern businesses are asking whether their customers can rent or lease their products instead of buying them outright – with the business keeping the same level of income or profit. This moves away from the built-in obsolescence seen often in products today (particularly tech), which is designed to encourage regular new purchases rather than lifetime use.

Consider this
- Do you accept that there is no such thing as waste in nature?
- How can you move from take-make-waste to a circular approach?
- What can you rent instead of buying?

Inspired by *The Sustainable Business Book*

STOP, THINK, CHALLENGE

ATTITUDE

ACTION

CREATIVITY

COMMUNICATION

EFFICIENCY

EMPATHY

STRATEGY

SUSTAINABILITY

I believe that sustainability is everyone's responsibility.

Sustainable thinking needs to permeate all aspects of life and business. If we all change our day-to-day behaviour, then we can make a significant difference.

To be clear, this is not a case of deviously handing the responsibility for the world's problems from the company to the individual in the same way that many argue that fossil fuel companies invented personal carbon calculators to make it look as though individuals were responsible for emissions rather than them. Instead, collective responsibility means making sure that people routinely stop, think and challenge everything they do.

STOP, THINK, CHALLENGE.
- **Is there a greener way of doing this?**
- **Is there a kinder way of doing this?**
- **Is there a more inclusive way of doing this?**
- **Is there a more thoughtful way of doing this?**

An entire cultural shift is needed to make sure that everything is consistently questioned through a sustainability lens.

For example, if everyone in an organisation instinctively challenges their purchasing on behalf of the company (and, indeed, at home), significant change can occur.

Responsible purchasing checklist	
Do we really need this?	
What is it made of?	
What is it wrapped in?	
Where is it coming from?	
Who made it?	
How will it be transported and delivered?	
Is it built to last?	
How will it be disposed of (where will it end up)?	
Is there a greener, more responsible option?	

Consider this
- Do you stop, think and challenge everything you do?
- Do you consider everything you purchase?
- Do you agree that sustainability is everyone's responsibility?

Inspired by *The Sustainable Business Book*

8.10 GREENWASH ALERT

I am conscious of greenwashing, both in terms of my own company's products and when buying products from other people.

It is natural for marketing people to have an overenthusiastic view of their brands, products or services. Who wants a Marketing Director who doesn't think their product is great?

There are certainly many examples of premeditated and well-orchestrated greenwashing in business today. But are the marketers always the villains here? Or is it sometimes simply a case of overenthusiasm, grabbing at claims and terminology that they believe their customers want to hear?

As custodians of a brand's reputation, marketers need to be wary, and not become complicit – however attractive a claim may sound. Some simple cross-examination early on can flush out the dubious, the doubtful and the delusional.

This framework can help anyone interrogate a proposed marketing claim. It encourages communicators to look at it from a legal perspective (legally, can we say this?) *and* a moral perspective (OK but, morally, should we say this?)

ATTITUDE

ACTION

CREATIVITY

COMMUNICATION

EFFICIENCY

EMPATHY

STRATEGY

SUSTAINABILITY

MARKETING CLAIM

1. LEGALLY, can we say this?

2. What is the source?

3. How has the evidence been validated?

4. Is the source independent and/or unbiased?

5. Who signed off the wording?

6. MORALLY, should we say this?

7. What are we potentially overstating?

8. Is this only part of the story? What is not being mentioned?

9. What could customers be wary of?

10. Are they right to be wary? How can we address this?

What needs to be ...

CHECKED?

CHALLENGED?

CLARIFIED?

CHANGED?

If in any doubt, you need to:
- CHECK the facts,
- CLARIFY the details,
- CHALLENGE like (your greenest) customer, and
- CHANGE where necessary

For your own purchasing integrity, you should also be challenging the marketing claims of green and sustainable products.

- Are the claims robust enough?
- Are they scientific?
- Are they using vague terms (like eco)?
- Are they focusing attention on one small element, while hiding the bad stuff in the background?
- Do I really trust this?

If in doubt, give it more scrutiny and ask more questions.

Consider this
- Do you avoid greenwashing?
- Do you challenge the products you sell?
- Do you challenge the products you buy?

Inspired by *The Sustainable Business Book*

ATTITUDE

ACTION

CREATIVITY

COMMUNICATION

EFFICIENCY

EMPATHY

STRATEGY

SUSTAINABILITY

"

If you don't ask, you don't get; you can't turn down what you haven't gone for.

"

Dr Dayne Beccano-Kelly,
Dementia researcher

PART FOUR

WHAT ALL THIS
MEANS FOR YOU

You will have noticed that the questions in the Aces self-audit are very different from other psychometric testing you may have come across. Many of those highlight your strengths and weaknesses, and the result leaves with you with the impression that you are a certain type. It is often implied that this is a permanent state, and you are then left to get on and deal with it, apparently remaining the same for the rest of your career.

We don't agree with this approach. There are no trick questions here, or ones that you would have trouble answering. They are just based on your confidence levels and personal understanding of what you feel you can do.

This means that, if you want to, you can change, and you can do it as many times as you like as you progress. In other words, you may originally have been a Persuasive Enactor but after improving your skills in certain areas, you have migrated to being a Thoughtful Inventor.

Following this new approach to self-improvement, you can continue to learn at whatever pace you like, particularly if you investigate the additional resources and further reading thoroughly.

We support the philosophy of continuous learning. Read, understand, improve, reflect, repeat. All of which will help you to be your best business self and lead to smart performance.

That's what this book is all about.

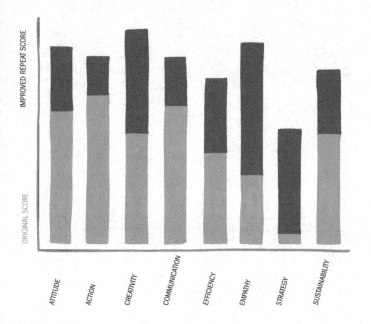

MOVING FROM:
A PERSUASIVE ENACTOR

TO:
A THOUGHTFUL INVENTOR

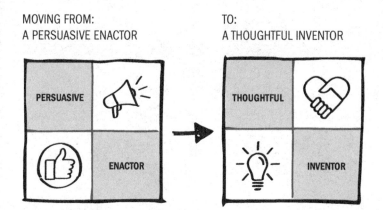

" Methods are the most powerful truths of all. "

Nietzsche,
Philosopher

PART FIVE

WHAT ALL THIS MEANS FOR BUSINESSES

The system in this book is primarily about individuals but, obviously, has significant application to whole businesses. Once a group of people have completed the self-audit, any company can gain a consistent overview of all the skills at their disposal. This immediately allows leaders, department heads, team leaders and HR directors to see whether the skills balance is appropriate for their business circumstances and where further training and development is needed.

Here are some examples of how the results can be applied.

BROAD OVERVIEW OF RANGE OF SKILLS IN A COMPANY

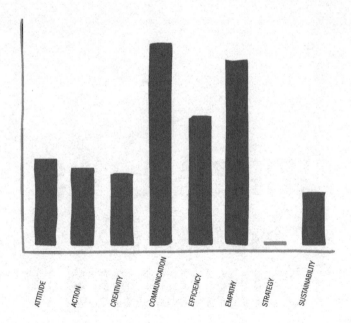

VIEW OF SPECIFIC INDIVIDUAL SKILLS ON A LEADERSHIP TEAM

Homing in on a more individual level can help inform who might be in the right or wrong roles, who needs additional skills development in specific areas, and where hiring may be needed to improve capability overall. This is particularly poignant when used for small groups, such as a leadership team.

The overview provides a visual guide to the balance in the team. Placing each individual in the relevant box that the system shows is their primary skill immediately reveals if the team is overequipped in certain areas or completely lacking in others.

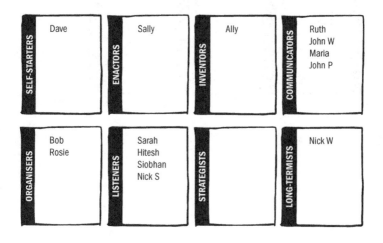

SELF-STARTERS
Dave

ENACTORS
Sally

INVENTORS
Ally

COMMUNICATORS
Ruth
John W
Maria
John P

ORGANISERS
Bob
Rosie

LISTENERS
Sarah
Hitesh
Siobhan
Nick S

STRATEGISTS

LONG-TERMISTS
Nick W

PRIMARY AND SECONDARY SKILLS TEAM OVERVIEW

Repeating this process to add secondary skills adds texture and shows where colleagues can complement or support each other, particularly when covering for illness, maternity or paternity leave, or overwhelming work demand overall.

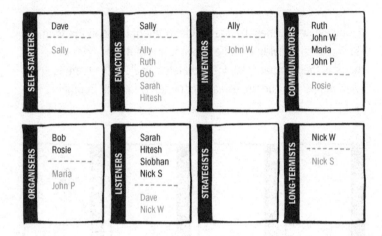

SELF-STARTERS
Dave

Sally

ENACTORS
Sally

Ally
Ruth
Bob
Sarah
Hitesh

INVENTORS
Ally

John W

COMMUNICATORS
Ruth
John W
Maria
John P

Rosie

ORGANISERS
Bob
Rosie

Maria
John P

LISTENERS
Sarah
Hitesh
Siobhan
Nick S

Dave
Nick W

STRATEGISTS

LONG-TERMISTS
Nick W

Nick S

SPECIFIC OVERVIEW OF A WHOLE COMPANY OR LARGE TEAM

A full profile analysis grid, using both the primary and secondary strengths of individuals, can also show where there is too much, too little or none of the skills needed to constitute a well-balanced and correctly skilled group. At a glance, this can provide a snapshot of whether a skill is unsuitably overrepresented or completely absent.

		HIGHEST SCORE – PRIMARY (BY NUMBER OF EMPLOYEES)								
		ATTITUDE	ACTION	CREATIVITY	COMMUNICATION	EFFICIENCY	EMPATHY	STRATEGY	SUSTAINABILITY	
SECOND HIGHEST SCORE – SECONDARY (BY NUMBER OF EMPLOYEES)	ATTITUDE		ME 3	MI	MC 1	MO 3	ML	MS	MLT 3	10
	ACTION	AOSS		AOI 2	AOC 4	AOO 3	AOL 3	AOS	AOLT	12
	CREATIVITY	CSS	CE		CC 3	CO	CL 3	CS	CLT	6
	COMMUNICATION	PeSS	PeE	PeI		PeO 1	PeL 1	PeS	PeLT	2
	EFFICIENCY	PrSS	PrE 3	PrI	PrC 4		PrL 1	PrS	PrLT	8
	EMPATHY	TSS 4	TE	TI	TC 3	TO		TS	TLT 2	9
	STRATEGY	SSS	SE	SI	SC	SO	SL		SLT	0
	SUSTAINABILITY	RSS	RE	RI 1	RC	RO 3	RL 1	RS		5
		4	6	3	15	10	9	0	10	

Here is a reminder of what the acronyms stand for. For the complete list of descriptors, see page 25.

AOC	=	Action-Orientated Communicator	**PrC**	=	Productive Communicator
AOI	=	Action-Orientated Inventor	**PrE**	=	Productive Enactor
AOL	=	Action-Orientated Listener	**PrI**	=	Productive Inventor
AOLT	=	Action-Orientated Long-Termist	**PrL**	=	Productive Listener
AOO	=	Action-Orientated Organiser	**PrLT**	=	Productive Long-Termist
AOSS	=	Action-Orientated Self-Starter	**PrSS**	=	Productive Self-Starter
AOS	=	Action-Orientated Strategist	**PrS**	=	Productive Strategist
CC	=	Creative Communicator	**RC**	=	Responsible Communicator
CE	=	Creative Enactor	**RE**	=	Responsible Enactor
CL	=	Creative Listener	**RI**	=	Responsible Inventor
CLT	=	Creative Long-Termist	**RL**	=	Responsible Listener
CO	=	Creative Organiser	**RO**	=	Responsible Organiser
CSS	=	Creative Self-Starter	**RSS**	=	Responsible Self-Starter
CS	=	Creative Strategist	**RS**	=	Responsible Strategist
MC	=	Motivated Communicator	**SC**	=	Strategic Communicator
ME	=	Motivated Enactor	**SE**	=	Strategic Enactor
MI	=	Motivated Inventor	**SI**	=	Strategic Inventor
ML	=	Motivated Listener	**SL**	=	Strategic Listener
MLT	=	Motivated Long-Termist	**SLT**	=	Strategic Long-Termist
MO	=	Motivated Organiser	**SO**	=	Strategic Organiser
MS	=	Motivated Strategist	**SSS**	=	Strategic Self-Starter
PeE	=	Persuasive Enactor	**TC**	=	Thoughtful Communicator
PeI	=	Persuasive Inventor	**TE**	=	Thoughtful Enactor
PeL	=	Persuasive Listener	**TI**	=	Thoughtful Inventor
PeLT	=	Persuasive Long-Termist	**TLT**	=	Thoughtful Long-Termist
PeO	=	Persuasive Organiser	**TO**	=	Thoughtful Organiser
PeSS	=	Persuasive Self-Starter	**TSS**	=	Thoughtful Self-Starter
PeS	=	Persuasive Strategist	**TS**	=	Thoughtful Strategist

SKILLS IMPROVEMENT TRACKED OVER TIME

Repeating the exercise after allowing time for individuals to work through the self-improvement material in this book or online can provide proof of progress and development, often much faster than instigating a conventional training programme.

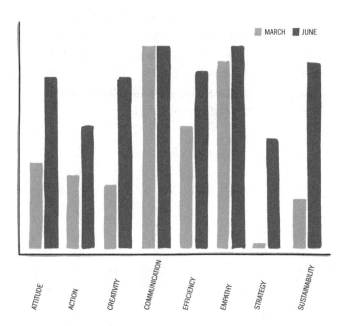

APPRAISALS TRANSFORMED DUE TO BOTH APPRAISER AND APPRAISEE USING THE SAME SKILLS CRITERIA

The system is very helpful for appraisals. Both the individual and their boss or line manager complete the assessment. The difference in perspective provides a consistent framework for appraisal discussions.

Instead of general action points that are frequently not followed up, the discussion can be followed by the signposted learning that the system provides automatically and immediately. The enthusiastic individual does not need to wait for any subsequent line manager action. They simply get on with their self-improvement material at their own speed.

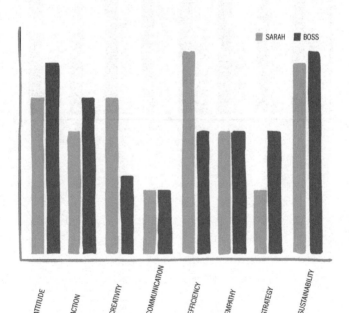

Examples of outcomes include:

1. There are a number of attributes on which the appraiser and the appraisee have given similar scores – they are in agreement. They can agree to agree.

2. There are a number of attributes where there is significant divergence – this is a case of "let's discuss it." Differences can be worked through and plans made.

3. Where the individual has 'overscored' an attribute, the appraiser should explain the difference and the reasons the individual needs to improve in that area.

4. Where the individual has 'underscored' an attribute, the appraiser can explain why others see them as having good skills in that area, thereby boosting confidence and providing motivating direction.

All in all, these outcomes are clearer and much more satisfactory than many appraisals that end inconclusively and do not always result in helpful action.

Visit **theACESsystem.com** for more details on The ACES System corporate packages and products.

"

You can work on something you don't have, or you can work on something you do have.

"

Michael Johnson,
Olympic athlete

PART SIX

ONLINE RESOURCES, SOURCES AND SUGGESTED FURTHER READING

ONLINE RESOURCES

In the online version, you receive a personalised report explaining your typology, showing a histogram of your skills, and a ten-page interactive PDF outlining your potential improvement areas and learning opportunities in every skills area (see Part II).

This directs you to the fastest possible route to microlearning materials, all based on your own assessment of your skills. You can then immediately choose to take self-improvement steps by accessing the library of material in the system.

There are 120 fast spreads to read, as in this book, 120 short audio clips, and additional suggestions for further reading. Those interested can, of course, buy the full versions of any of the books from which the material is drawn. Summaries of most of the books mentioned can be found on: greatesthitsblog.com.

SOURCES BY SKILLS AREA

Attitude

The Excellence Book, Kevin and Rosie Duncan (LID, 2023)
The Intelligent Work Book, Kevin Duncan (LID, 2020)
An Optimist's Tour of the Future, Mark Stevenson (Profile, 2012)
Gig: The Life and Times of a Rock-star Fantasist, Simon Armitage (Penguin, 2009)
#Now, Max McKeown (Aurum Press, 2016)
The Empath's Survival Guide, Judith Orloff (Sounds True, 2018)

Action

The Smart Thinking Book, Kevin Duncan (LID, 2021)
The Diagrams Book, Kevin Duncan (LID, 2018)
Brand Manners, Hamish Pringle and William Gordon (Wiley, 2003)
Decisive, Chip and Dan Heath (Random House, 2013)
Essentialism, Greg McKeown (Virgin Books, 2014)
Stuffocation, James Wallman (Penguin Life, 2017)

The Life-Changing Magic of Tidying, Marie Kondo (Vermillion, 2014)
The Pirate Inside, Adam Morgan (John Wiley, 2004)
The Subtle Art of Not Giving A F*ck, Mark Manson (Harper One, 2016)
Toward a Psychology of Awakening, John Welwood (Shambhala Publications, 2002)

Creativity

The Ideas Book, Kevin Duncan (LID, 2019)
The Smart Strategy Book, Kevin Duncan (LID, 2022)
Contagious, Jonah Berger (Simon & Schuster, 2013)
Eating the Big Fish, Adam Morgan (John Wiley, 1999)
How to Kill a Unicorn, Mark Payne (Nicholas Brealey, 2014)
Thinking, Fast and Slow, Daniel Kahneman (Allen Lane, 2011)

Communication

The Bullshit-Free Book, Kevin Duncan (LID, 2022)
The Smart Thinking Book, Kevin Duncan (LID, 2021)
Authentic Marketing, Larry Weber (John Wiley, 2019)
Brief, Joseph McCormack (Wiley, 2014)
Business Bullshit, André Spicer (Routledge, 2018)
Calling Bullshit, Carl T. Bergstrom and Jevin D. West (Allen Lane, 2020)
On Bullshit, Harry G. Frankfurt (Harvard Business Review Press, 2005)
The Salesperson's Secret Code, Ian Mills, Mark Ridley, Ben Laker and Tim Chapman (LID, 2017)

Efficiency

The Intelligent Work Book, Kevin Duncan (LID, 2020)
The Diagrams Book, Kevin Duncan (LID, 2018)
Great by Choice, Collins and Hansen (2011)
Radical Candor, Kim Scott (Pan Macmillan, 2017)
The Feedback Book, Dawn Sillett (LID, 2016)
The Inner Game of Tennis, Tim Gallwey (Pan, 2015)

Empathy

The Ethical Business Book, Sarah Duncan (LID, 2019)
The Sustainable Business Book, Kevin and Sarah Duncan (LID, 2023)
Clever, Goffee and Jones (Harvard Business Press, 2009)
Diversify, June Sarpong (HQ, 2017)
The Five Dysfunctions of a Team, Patrick Lencioni, (Jossey-Bass, 2002)
The Language of Leaders, Kevin Murray (Kogan Page, 2012)
To Sell Is Human, Daniel Pink (Canongate, 2012)

Strategy

The Smart Strategy Book, Kevin Duncan (LID, 2022)
The Excellence Book, Kevin and Rosie Duncan (LID, 2023)

Business Genius, James Bannerman (Pearson, 2014)
Essentialism, Greg McKeown (Virgin Books, 2014)
Great by Choice, Jim Collins and Morten T. Hansen (2011)
Playing to Win, Alan G. Lafley and Roger Martin (Harvard Business Review Press, 2013)
The Challenger Sale, Matthew Dixon and Brent Adamson (Portfolio Penguin, 2011)
The Strategy Book, Max McKeown (Pearson, 2012)
To Sell Is Human, Daniel Pink (Canongate, 2012)

Sustainability
The Sustainable Business Book, Kevin and Sarah Duncan (LID, 2023)
The Ethical Business Book, Sarah Duncan (LID, 2019)
A Life on our Planet, David Attenborough (Witness Books, 2020)
Conscious Capitalism Field Guide, Raj Sisodia, Timothy Henry and Thomas Eckschmidt (Harvard Business Review Press, 2018)
Green Swans, John Elkington (Fast Company Press, 2020)
How Bad Are Bananas?, Mike Berners-Lee (Profile, 2020)
How to Avoid a Climate Disaster, Bill Gates (Allen Lane, 2021)
How to Save our Planet, Mark Maslin (Penguin Life, 2021)
Sustainable Business: A One-Planet Approach, Sally Jeanrenaud, Jean-Paul Jeanrenaud and Jonathan Gosling (John Wiley, 2016)
There Is No Planet B, Mike Berners-Lee (Cambridge University Press, 2019)

BY THE AUTHORS
The Bullshit-Free Book, Kevin Duncan (LID, 2018)
The Business Bullshit Book, Kevin Duncan (LID, 2016)
The Diagrams Book, Kevin Duncan (LID, 2018)
The Ethical Business Book, Sarah Duncan (LID, 2019)
The Excellence Book, Kevin and Rosie Duncan (LID, 2023)
The Ideas Book, Kevin Duncan (LID, 2019)
The Intelligent Work Book, Kevin Duncan (LID, 2020)
The Smart Strategy Book, Kevin Duncan (LID, 2022)
The Smart Thinking Book, Kevin Duncan (LID, 2021)
The Sustainable Business Book, Kevin and Sarah Duncan (LID, 2023)

SUGGESTED FURTHER READING BY SKILLS AREA
Attitude
Atomic Habits, James Clear (Random House Business, 2018)
Drive, Daniel Pink (Canongate, 2009)
Happy Mind, Happy Life, Dr Rangan Chaterjee (Penguin Life, 2022)

Mastery, Robert Greene (Profile, 2012)
Messy, Tim Harford, (Little Brown, 2016)
The Advantage, Patrick Lencioni (Josey-Bass, 2012)
The Power of Now, Eckhart Tolle (Yellow Kite, 2001)
Why Has Nobody Told Me This Before? Dr Julie Smith (Michael Joseph, 2022)

Action
Commitment-led Marketing, Hofmeyr and Rice (John Wiley, 2001)
Left Brain, Right Stuff, Phil Rosenzweig (Profile, 2014)
Linchpin, Seth Godin (Piatkus, 2010)
The Decisive Moment, Jonah Lehrer (Canongate, 2009)
The E Myth Revisited, Michael E. Gerber (Harper Collins, 1995)
The Effortless Experience, Dixon, Toman and Delisi (Portfolio Penguin, 2013)
Thinking in New Boxes, Luc de Brabandere and Alan Iny (Random House, 2013)
Too Fast to Think, Chris Lewis (Kogan Page, 2016)

Creativity
Copy, Copy, Copy, Mark Earls (Wiley, 2015)
Creative Blindness, Dave Trott (Harriman House, 2019)
Flicking Your Creative Switch, Wayne Lotherington (John Wiley, 2003)
Frugal Innovation, Navi Radjou and Jaideep Prabhu (Economist Books, 2015)
Imagine, Jonah Lehrer (Canongate, 2012)
Making Ideas Happen, Scott Belsky (Portfolio, 2010)
One Plus One Equals Three, Dave Trott (Macmillan, 2015)
Outliers, Malcolm Gladwell (Little Brown, 2008)
Predatory Thinking, Dave Trott (Macmillan, 2013)
Sticky Wisdom, Kingdon et al. (Capstone, 2002)
The Accidental Creative, Todd Henry (Portfolio Penguin, 2011)
The Art of Creative Thinking, John Adair (Kogan Page, 1990)
The Brand Gap, Marty Neumeier (New Riders, 2006)
The First Mile, Scott D. Anthony (Harvard Business Review Press, 2014)
The Innovation Book, Max McKeown (Pearson, 2014)
The Science of Serendipity, Matt Kingdon (John Wiley, 2012)
Where Good Ideas Come From, Steven Johnson (Penguin, 2010)

Communication
A Field Guide to Lies And Statistics, Daniel Levitin (Penguin, 2016)
Bad Language, Graham Edmonds (Southbank, 2008)
No Bullshit Leadership, Chris Hirst (Profile Books, 2019)
Politics and the English Language, George Orwell (Penguin 2013)
Talk Lean, Alan Palmer (Wiley, 2014)
The Language Wars, Henry Hitchings (John Murray, 2011)
The Life-Changing Science of Detecting Bullshit, John V. Petrocelli (St. Martin's Press, 2021)

The Prevalence of Humbug, Max Black (Cornell University Press, 1983)
Through The Language Glass, Guy Deutscher (Arrow, 2011)
Why Business People Speak Like Idiots, Brian Fugere, Chelsea Hardaway and Jon Warshawsky (Free Press, 2005)

Efficiency
Big Bang Disruption, Downes and Nunes (Portfolio Penguin, 2014)
Never Split the Difference, Chris Voss (Random House, 2016)
Simply Brilliant, Fergus O'Connell (Pearson, 2001)
Smarter Faster Better, Charles Duhigg (Random House, 2016)
Start with Why, Simon Sinek (Portfolio Penguin, 2009)
Surrounded by Psychopaths, Thomas Erikson (Vermilion, 2017)
The Ideal Team Player, Patrick Lencioni, (Jossey-Bass, 2016)
The Organised Mind, Daniel Levitin (Penguin, 2015)
The Stupidity Paradox, Alvesson and Spicer (Profile, 2016)

Empathy
Flow, Mihaly Csikszentmihalyi (Rider, 2002)
Nudge, Thaler and Sunstein (Caravan, 2008)
The Ethical Capitalist, Julian Richer (Random House, 2018)
The Ethical Leader, Morgen Witzel (Bloomsbury, 2018)
The Geography of Thought, Richard Nisbett (Nicholas Brealey, 2003)
The Infinite Game, Simon Sinek (Penguin, 2019)
The Joy of Work, Bruce Daisley (Random House, 2019)
When Cultures Collide, Richard Lewis (Nicholas Brealey, 2005)
Why Should Anyone Work Here?, Rob Goffee and Gareth Jones (Harvard Business Review Press, 2015)

Strategy
A Beautiful Constraint, Morgan and Barden (Wiley, 2015)
Antifragile, Nassim Nicholas Taleb (Allen Lane, 2012)
Business Ethics, Andrew Crane, Dirk Matten, Sarah Glozer, Laura Spence (Oxford University Press, 2016)
Business Is Beautiful, Danet et al. (LID, 2013)
Conscious Leadership, Mackey, McIntosh, Cripps (Portfolio Penguin, 2020)
Consumer.ology, Philip Graves (Nicholas Brealey, 2013)
Conversations that Win the Complex Sale, Erik Peterson and Tim Riesterer (McGraw Hill, 2011)
David and Goliath, Malcolm Gladwell, Penguin Allen Lane, 2013)
Decoded, Phil Barden (John Wiley, 2013)
Execution, Larry Bossidy and Ram Charan (Crown Business, 2002)
Factfulness, Hans Rosling (Sceptre, 2019)

Inside the Box, Drew Boyd and Jacob Goldenberg (Profile, 2013)
Leaders Eat Last, Simon Sinek (Portfolio Penguin, 2014)
Leadership BS, Jeffrey Pfeffer (Harper Business, 2015)
The Long Tail, Chris Anderson (Random House, 2006)
The Silo Effect, Gillian Tett (Little Brown, 2015)
Uncommon Sense, Common Nonsense, Jules Goddard and Tony Eccles (Profile, 2012)

Sustainability
50 Ways to Help The Planet, Sian Berry (Kyle Books, 2018)
All In, David Grayson, Chris Coulter and Mark Lee (Routledge 2018)
Better, John Grant (Unbound, 2018)
Climate Change: A Very Short introduction, Mark Maslin (Oxford University Press, 2021)
Climate Change and the Road to Net Zero, Mathew Hampshire-Waugh
(Crowstone Publishing, 2021)
Compassion Inc, Gaurav Sinha (Ebury Press, 2018)
Doughnut Economics, Kate Raworth (Random House, 2017)
Economics for a Fragile Planet, Edward Barbier (Cambridge University Press, 2022)
Ethical Marketing and the New Consumer, Chris Arnold (John Wiley, 2009)
False Alarm, Bjorn Lomborg (Basic, 2020)
Good Is the New Cool, Afdhel Aziz and Bobby Jones (Regan Arts, 2016)
Greener Marketing, John Grant (Wiley, 2020)
Humane Capital, Vlatka Hlupic (Bloomsbury, 2019)
Natural Capital, Dieter Helm (Yale University Press 2015)
Net Positive, Paul Polman and Andrew Winston (Harvard Business Review Press, 2021)
Net Zero, Dieter Helm (William Collins, 2020)
No One Is too Small to Make a Difference, Greta Thunberg (Penguin, 2019)
Our Final Warning, Mark Lynas (4th Estate, 2020)
Sustainable Marketing, Michelle Carvill, Gemma Butler and Geraint Evans (Bloomsbury, 2021)
The Future We Choose, Christiana Figueres and Tom Rivett-Carnac (Manilla Press, 2020)
The Joyful Environmentalist, Isabel Losada (Watkins, 2020)
The New Brand Spirit, Christian Conrad and Marjorie Ellis Thompson (Gower Publishing, 2013)
The New Climate War, Michael E. Mann (Scribe, 2021)
The New Rules of Green Marketing, Jacquelyn Ottman (Greenleaf, 2010)
The Performance Economy, Walter Stahel (Palgrave Macmillan, 2010)
The Sustainable Business, Jonathan T. Scott (Greenleaf, 2013)
The Sustainable Business Handbook, David Grayson, Chris Coulter and Mark Lee
(Kogan Page, 2022)
The Uninhabitable Earth, David Wallace-Wells (Allen Lane, 2019)
Volt Rush, Henry Sanderson (Oneworld, 2022)
We Are the Weather, Jonathan Safran Foer (Penguin, 2019)
WEconomy, Craig Kielburger, Holly Branson and Marc Kielburger (John Wiley, 2018)
Who Cares Wins, David Jones (Pearson, 2012)

ABOUT THE AUTHORS

KEVIN DUNCAN and **SARAH DUNCAN** have combined forces to produce a book to help anyone improve their skills. Kevin is the UK's bestselling business author, and Sarah brings her expertise through the design of the ACES System, which consolidates the best writing of both authors in one place for the first time.

ISBN: 978-1-911687-53-5

ISBN: 978-1-915951-03-8

ISBN: 978-1-911687-80-1

ISBN: 978-1-915951-07-6

ISBN: 978-1-911687-54-2

ISBN: 978-1-911687-96-2